INTERMITTENT FASTING FOR WOMEN OVER 50

The Winning Formula To Lose Weight, Unlock Metabolism And Rejuvenate. It Only Takes A Few Hours Without Food To Obtain Immediate Results.

|2021 Edition|

Legal & Disclaimer

Upon using the contents and information contained in this book, you agree to hold harmless the Author from and against any damages, costs, and expenses, including any legal fees potentially resulting from the application of any of the information provided by this book. This disclaimer applies to any loss, damages or injury caused by the use and application, whether directly or indirectly, of any advice or information presented, whether for breach of contract, tort, negligence, personal injury, criminal intent, or under any other cause of action.

You agree to accept all risks of using the information presented inside this book.

You agree that by continuing to read this book, where appropriate and/or necessary, you shall consult a professional (including but not limited to your doctor, attorney, or financial advisor or such other advisor as needed) before using any of the suggested remedies, techniques, or information in this book.

Introduction

This book contains all the essential information you need to know about fasting.

Simply put, fasting means not eating any food for a given period of time. It may seem like anybody could do it on their own without having to refer to medical experts or even a guide book. However, fasting is not as easy as it sounds.

There are several nuances to it that can spell the difference between a successful fast and a failed attempt. Even the tiniest tweaks to your fasting plan can enhance or diminish the benefits that you could get from a fast.

In this book, you will learn about:

- ✓ What is intermittent fasting?
- ✓ Intermittent fasting types for women over 50.
- ✓ Nutrition for women over 50 and hormonal problems
- ✓ What to Eat While Intermittent Fasting for woman OVER 50
- ✓ How IF Affects Women at This Age & How to Approach It
- ✓ Benefits Of If For Women Over 50
- ✓ Tips And Trick For Women Over 50

10

✓ Exercises to Lose Weight After 50 Years Old
✓ Recipes for fasting for women over 50 years

This book aims to guide in discovering the best fasting method for you, as well as ease you into the process of abstaining from food in a healthy manner. Fasting can be quite challenging, but with commitment and discipline, you can be sure that the rewards would be great.

CHAPTER ONE

HOW INTERMITTENT FASTING WORKS: Who Can Benefit from Fasting

Fasting is highly recommended for anyone who wishes to live a longer and healthier life. Many medical experts also recognize this as an excellent way to manage and reverse several chronic health conditions, such as heart diseases and cancer. However, studies show that fasting may not be effective for all types of people.

As with any major health decision that you have to make, it is best to seek first the professional opinion of your physician before committing yourself to significant changes in your lifestyle and diet. Fasting may aggravate any existing health condition, especially the ones that you may not be aware of at this point.

Have an open discussion with your doctor about your goals for fasting, as well as the probable side-effects this activity could have on your health. By doing so, you would be able to engage in fasting without any serious reservations about your wellbeing.

For your reference, here is a rundown of specific groups of people, and their respective likelihood of benefiting from fasting:

Children

Average children, up to the age of 18, are not recommended to fast. At most, health experts may advise parents to control the frequency of their child's meals throughout the day. Children should not be abstaining from food for long periods of time. The nutrition they gain from their meals are essential for their growth and development.

Even overweight children are not exempted from this. Parents, with the guidance of the child's pediatrician or a nutritionist, should try restructuring first the child's diet. The objective for such a move is to prevent the child from consuming junk food and too much sugar, and replace them with healthier options.

Once the overweight child begins eating a well-balanced diet, most parents do not have any reason left to wonder if child has to go through a fast to lose the excess weight.

If you still think that a child below the age of 18 would benefit from a fast, you should consult with the child's physician first.

Healthy Adults

Being in good health does not exclude healthy adults from benefiting from fasting. In fact, going into a fast from time to time may be helpful in sustaining their current health condition.

High-Level Athletes

Several benefits of fasting are attractive for many athletes. Fasting enables the body to recover faster from being strained, and it improves the absorption of nutrients of the digestive system. Both benefits are critical in the process of developing muscles and increasing physical strength.

Athletes should take extra care when adapting fasting into their normal routines. Experts do not suggest going on a fast right before and during game days. Fasting should not also be done when the athlete has to engage in intense and extended practice sessions. Doing any of these would seriously deplete them to the point that the continual act of abstaining from food becomes harmful to their health.

Pregnant Women

Multiple studies have been conducted on the effects of fasting among pregnant Muslim women during Ramadan. To date, researchers have found that fasting has no negative effects on the mother or the child.

Pregnancy, however, is a highly sensitive state, so pregnant women are encouraged to get the approval of their respective doctors first before entering a fast.

Vegetarians or Vegans

Fasting is compatible with almost every type of lifestyle or diet. Due to the dietary restrictions of vegetarians and vegans, the effects of fasting may even be enhanced when implemented properly.

Individuals with Type-2 Diabetes

Fasting has long been used by medical experts as a method of reversing Type-2 Diabetes. Various research studies on this strategy show consistent results indicating the positive effects of fasting to diabetic people. Still, if you are diabetic too, you should consult first with your doctor before adapting any form of fasting.

Individuals who are Immunosuppressed

People who are suffering from HIV, AIDS, lupus, different types of cancer, or any similar disorders related to the immune system should seek the opinion of their physicians before making any major lifestyle or dietary changes, such as fasting.

Though fasting is largely beneficial to most people, it may wreak havoc to the delicate balance of bodily chemicals and processes of an immunosuppressed individual.

Individuals with Eating Disorders

An eating disorder is rooted upon the physical, mental, and emotional aspects of a person suffering from it. Therefore, there is no guarantee that fasting may help resolve these food-related issues. Those who have been diagnosed with eating disorders should get the approval of their psychotherapists first before applying the principles of fasting into their lives.

As you can see, almost every group of people may benefit from fasting. However, most groups are also encouraged to get the opinion of medical experts prior to making a commitment to fasting.

In case you want to do a preliminary self-assessment before your consultation, here is a set of guide questions that you may reflect upon to determine whether or not fasting is for you.

- How well do handle hunger pangs?

- Can you fully commit to fasting for at least three months?

- Do you think you have the physical and mental fortitude to last through an entire fasting period?

- How would you describe your current diet?

- How would you describe your current lifestyle?

- How do you regard the thought of having to exercise regularly?

- Do you have support system who can motivate you and hold you accountable while you are fasting?

16

It is best if you would write down your answers to these questions in a personal journal. Refer to your responses before making a final decision regarding fasting. Even if your physician has given you clearance to pursue with this, you must be willing to commit yourself, and go through the highs and lows of fasting as best you can.

Take the time to reflect upon the questions given above. Doing so would help you figure out if you have what it takes to reap the numerous benefits of fasting.

There is no point in the known human history wherein the concept of fasting has not existed in some shape or form. The voluntary act of abstaining from food, drink, or a luxury has deep roots in different cultures and religions around the world. Each form may vary in some way, but the core principles of fasting remain consistent.

Even the motivations behind each variation tend to be of similar natures. For some, fasting is a way to heal the body and the mind. Most religions, on the other hand, believe it is way of strengthening the spirit and one's connection to a divine being.

To better illustrate the universality of fasting across time and location, here are the important historical highlights that would give you a better picture of the practice of fasting across different cultures and religions.

- One of the earliest records of fasting show that a number of prominent ancient Greek figures were believers. For example, Pythagoras, a legendary Greek philosopher and mathematician, followed a 40-day starvation cycle in order to enhance his creativity and mental clarity.

  The father of modern medicine, Hippocrates, was among the first to recognize the applications of fasting to the medical field. His observations of the human body had led

18

him to a conclusion that a sick body would benefit from the absence of food.

Ancient Greek healers had also observed that the frequency of epileptic seizures was lower among patients who were engaging in a fast at the time compared those who were not.

- Some ancient cultures, such as the Natives from North America, believed that fasting before a war would ensure their success in battle. They had also engaged in fasting to prevent the occurrence of wide-scale catastrophes like famine and drought.

- Both the Old Testament and the New Testament of the Bible mention several instances of fasting. Even Jesus Christ himself had fasted for 40 days and 40 nights in a desert. Other Biblical figures who have also fasted include Moses, Elijah, and Paul, one of Jesus' apostles.

Given its presence in the Bible, the Christian church encourages its followers to participate in a 40-day fast before Easter as a form of repentance. Though the exact date on which this practice had first been adapted is unknown, the fasting guidelines imposed among Christians have become more lenient throughout the years.

- Muslims practice fasting since it is one of the Five Pillars of Islam—the others being (1) pilgrimage, (2) prayer, (3) declaration of faith, and (4) charity. They believe that through fasting, they would become closer to Allah become it begins with a spiritual intention. Furthermore, fasting fosters solidarity among Muslims who are also fasting, and amplifies feelings of compassion and empathy towards those who are suffering.

  These beliefs culminate during Ramadan, a Muslim holiday that is characterized by a month-long period of fasting. During this time, all Muslims are prohibited from consuming food while there is daylight.

- Buddhist monks and nuns abide by the rules of Vinyana, wherein it is stated that followers should not eat anything after they had taken their meals at noon. However, the followers themselves do not consider this as a form of fasting. Instead, they think of it as a part of their normal routine.

- The fasting days among Hindus differ depending on which deity they are following. For example, Vishnu requires fasting on a Thursday, while followers of Shiva fast on a Monday. Hindus also engage in monthly fasting periods that occur after certain lunar phases.

There are also individuals who perform complete or partial fasting as part of a religious practice called Vratas. Aside from abstaining from food and/or water, those who are practicing it are required to observe personal hygiene, celibacy, and honesty, among others.

- The traditional form of Judaism includes a requirement of 6 fasting days within a given year among its followers. The fasting day lasts from sunset of a particular day up to the sunset of the succeeding day.

- Jains believe that fasting regulates the demands of their bodies, eliminates their accumulated bad karma, and rejuvenates their spirits. As such, they make it a point to incorporate fasting into their day to day lives. Aside from abstaining from food and water, Jains are also required to worship their gods, serve Jain monks and nuns, and engage in acts of charity while fasting.

- A secular fasting holiday in Geneva, Switzerland called the "Jeune Genevois" originated in the Middle Ages. During that period, the people dedicated certain days of the year for fasting as a form of penitence whenever they experienced epidemics, wars, and other big-scale calamities.

As shown through these examples of fasting traditions, fasting had been in existence for hundreds of years, and will continue to be practiced across the world in the foreseeable future. Fasting has also undergone evolution throughout the years. Though most practitioners perform it as a part of their religious beliefs, a growing number of health enthusiasts have recognized the benefits of fasting on their health.

If you are not fasting due to your religion, then you may still practice fasting according to your current lifestyle, personal preferences, and fitness goals. To guide you through this, the next section of this book covers the various modern ways of fasting that you may consider doing.

CHAPTER TWO: Intermittent fasting types for women over 50.

More About Intermittent Fasting Methods

There are several different ways of doing intermittent fasting — all of which involve splitting the day or week into eating and fasting periods.

During the fasting periods, you eat either very little or nothing at all.

Intermittent fasting has been very trendy in recent years. It is claimed to cause weight loss, improve metabolic health and perhaps even extend lifespan. Not surprisingly given the popularity, several different types/methods of intermittent fasting have been devised. All of them can be effective, but which one fits best will depend on the individual.

1. The 16/8 Method: Fast for 16 hours each day.

The 16/8 Method involves fasting every day for 14-16 hours, and restricting your daily "eating window" to 8-10 hours. Within the eating window, you can fit in 2, 3 or more meals.

This method is also known as the Leangains protocol, and was popularized by fitness expert Martin Berkhan.

Doing this method of fasting can actually be as simple as not eating anything after dinner, and skipping breakfast.

For example, if you finish your last meal at 8 pm and then don't eat until 12 noon the next day, then you are technically fasting for 16 hours between meals.

It is generally recommended that women only fast 14-15 hours, because they seem to do better with slightly shorter fasts. For people who get hungry in the morning and like to eat breakfast, then this can be hard to get used to at first. However, many breakfast skippers actually instinctively eat this way. You can drink water, coffee and other non-caloric beverages during the fast, and this can help reduce hunger levels. It is very important to eat mostly healthy foods during your eating window. This won't work if you eat lots of junk food or excessive amounts of calories.

I personally find this to be the most "natural" way to do intermittent fasting. I eat this way myself and find it to be 100% effortless.

I eat a low-carb diet, so my appetite is blunted somewhat. I simply do not feel hungry until around 1 pm in the afternoon. Then I eat my last meal around 6-9 pm, so I end up fasting for 16-19 hours.

NOTICE:
The 16/8 method involves daily fasts of 16 hours for men, and 14-15 hours for women. On each day, you restrict your eating to an 8-10 hour "eating window" where you can fit in 2-3 or more meals.

2. The 5:2 Diet: Fast for 2 days per week.

The 5:2 diet involves eating normally 5 days of the week, while restricting calories to 500-600 on two days of the week.

This diet is also called the Fast diet, and was popularized by British journalist and doctor Michael Mosley.

On the fasting days, it is recommended that women eat 500 calories, and men 600 calories.

For example, you might eat normally on all days except Mondays and Thursdays, where you eat two small meals (250 calories per meal for women, and 300 for men).

As critics correctly point out, there are no studies testing the 5:2 diet itself, but there are plenty of studies on the benefits of intermittent fasting.

NOTICE:
The 5:2 diet, or the Fast diet, involves eating 500-600 calories for two days of the week, but eating normally the other 5 days.

3. Eat-Stop-Eat: Do a 24-hour fast, once or twice a week.

Eat-Stop-Eat involves a 24-hour fast, either once or twice per week.

This method was popularized by fitness expert Brad Pilon, and has been quite popular for a few years. By fasting from dinner one day, to dinner the next, this amounts to a 24-hour fast. For example, if you finish dinner on Monday at 7 pm, and don't eat until dinner the next day at 7 pm, then you've just done a full 24-hour fast. You can also fast from breakfast to breakfast, or lunch

26

to lunch. The end result is the same. Water, coffee and other non-caloric beverages are allowed during the fast, but no solid food. If you are doing this to lose weight, then it is very important that you eat normally during the eating periods. As in, eat the same amount of food as if you hadn't been fasting at all.

The problem with this method is that a full 24-hour fast can be fairly difficult for many people.

However, you don't need to go all-in right away, starting with 14-16 hours and then moving upwards from there is fine. I've personally done this a few times. I found the first part of the fast very easy, but in the last few hours I did become ravenously hungry. I needed to apply some serious self-discipline to finish the full 24-hours and often found myself giving up and eating dinner a bit earlier.

Eat-Stop-Eat is an intermittent fasting program with one or two 24-hour fasts per week.

4. Alternate-Day Fasting: Fast every other day.

Alternate-Day fasting means fasting every other day.

There are several different versions of this. Some of them allow about 500 calories during the fasting days. Many of the lab studies showing health benefits of intermittent fasting used some version of this. A full fast every other day seems rather

27

extreme, so I do not recommend this for beginners. With this method, you will be going to bed very hungry several times per week, which is not very pleasant and probably unsustainable in the long-term.

Alternate-day fasting means fasting every other day, either by not eating anything or only eating a few hundred calories.

4.   The Warrior Diet: Fast during the day, eat a huge meal at night.

The Warrior Diet was popularized by fitness expert Ori Hofmekler. It involves eating small amounts of raw fruits and vegetables during the day, then eating one huge meal at night. Basically, you "fast" all day and "feast" at night within a 4 hour eating window.

The Warrior Diet was one of the first popular "diets" to include a form of intermittent fasting. This diet also emphasizes food choices that are quite similar to a paleo diet - whole, unprocessed foods that resemble what they looked like in nature.

The Warrior Diet is about eating only small amounts of vegetables and fruits during the day, then eating one huge meal at night.

5. Spontaneous Meal Skipping: Skip meals when convenient.

You don't actually need to follow a structured intermittent fasting plan to reap some of the benefits. Another option is to simply skip meals from time to time, when you don't feel hungry or are too busy to cook and eat. It is a myth that people need to eat every few hours or they will hit "starvation mode" or lose muscle. The human body is well equipped to handle long periods of famine, let alone missing one or two meals from time to time. So if you're really not hungry one day, skip breakfast and just eat a healthy lunch and dinner. Or if you're travelling somewhere and can't find anything you want to eat, do a short fast. Skipping 1 or 2 meals when you feel so inclined is basically a spontaneous intermittent fast. Just make sure to eat healthy foods at the other meals.

Another more "natural" way to do intermittent fasting is to simply skip 1 or 2 meals when you don't feel hungry or don't have time to eat.

A person's nutrition after 50 is crucial. It is, arguably, the most important factor in maintaining a healthy body at this age. It cannot withstand much more abuse in the form of fast food, inactivity and too much alcohol. The side effects are imminent.

Good nutrition is essential throughout the entire lifespan, of course, but around and after age 50, changes occur within the body that make the food you consume of particular significance, says Amy Gorin, MS, RDN, owner of Amy Gorin Nutrition in the New York City area.

"As you age, you lose muscle mass, about 10 percent each decade after age 45 she says. "While you're losing muscle, you're more likely to gain body fat and require less calories." This is because muscle burns more calories than body fat, she adds.

It's also important to prioritize exercise—in particular, resistance training to help counteract that decline in metabolism that happens with aging, Gorin says.

You have to prioritize nutrition to prevent heart disease, diabetes, and other conditions that are of greater concern as people get older.

Eat: Fatty fish

"Having at least two 3.5-ounce servings of cooked fatty fish such as salmon, tuna, or herring each week can help keep your heart health strong Gorin says. These fish provide heart-helping omega-3 fatty acids. They are essential to a person's overall health and they are promoted for their protective effects, especially on the brain, heart and eyes.

Eat: Prunes

Bone health is important as you get older. About a third of women and 20 percent of men over age 50 will break a bone because of osteoporosis, Gorin says. "Eating prunes helps to strengthen bone health and keep your bones healthy." In fact, she adds, eating five to six prunes daily has been shown to help prevent bone loss, per a study in Osteoporosis International." You can snack on prunes, add them to a salad, or make jam or even brownies with them."

Eat: Tomato Sauce

Surprisingly, this food helps prevent wrinkles, Gorin says. "Tomatoes are red gems that provide the antioxidant lycopene." This antioxidant can help protect skin from wrinkles and other damage that happens due to UV light, she adds. Cooked tomatoes are preferred because your body best absorbs the lycopene from them. You can add tomato sauce to pasta or use it in a spaghetti squash recipe.

Limit: Added Sugars

All people should limit intake of added sugar, and this is even more important as you get older, Gorin says. "Added sugar such as table sugar and brown sugar should make up no more than 10 percent of your total calories." So for a 2,000-calorie daily diet, that comes out to about 12 teaspoons of added sugar. "For the added sugar you are adding to your day, I recommend using one that offers some nutrition. My favorite is pure maple syrup." It's a unique sweetener because it boasts 60-plus health-helping polyphenols, as well as the blood-sugar-helping mineral manganese and the B vitamin riboflavin, she adds. "I like to use it to lightly sweeten overnight grains, a muffin recipe, or maple-Dijon salad dressing."

Don't eat: Trans Fats

Although you want to avoid these at all times, doing so is even more important as you get older. Before menopause, estrogen provides some protection against heart disease. "But after menopause, women are at a heightened risk for heart disease—and trans fats do not help the case!" Gorin says. "They can raise your 'bad' LDL cholesterol, lower your 'good' HDL cholesterol, and increase your risk of heart disease." Avoid them by reading ingredient labels to ensure that partially hydrogenated oil is not an ingredient.

They affect your heart, your immune system and even your bladder.

Change of Heart

The incidence of heart attack in women increases significantly after they reach menopause. Estrogen helps keep arteries pliable, and its decline may explain why blood pressure and LDL, or bad cholesterol, tend to rise during this time, says Deborah Kwon, MD, a cardiologist at the Cleveland Clinic. In addition, late peri- and postmenopause are associated with greater fat deposits around the heart, which has been linked to an increased risk (up to 54 percent) of heart disease, according to a 2015 study.

Healthy habit: Blast away ab flab. The fat that forms in your middle is especially toxic: "It produces compounds such as inflammatory proteins called cytokines, which have been linked to insulin resistance and type 2 diabetes as well as heart disease explains Scott Isaacs, MD, an endocrinologist and adjunct instructor at Emory University School of Medicine. One possible solution is to start hormone therapy, but timing may be key. "If you go on HT while you're experiencing perimenopause, it can help protect you from developing this bigger belly. But if you wait until you've passed menopause, it may be too late says Deborah Clegg, PhD, a professor of biomedical sciences at Cedars-Sinai in

Los Angeles. If you can't take HT or prefer not to, focus on committing to regular exercise and eating a diet low in sugar and saturated fat and rich in fruits, vegetables, whole grains, nuts, fish, and lean protein.

Oops, I Did It Again

Urinary incontinence peaks around menopause, with studies suggesting that between 30 and 40 percent of women in middle age experience some form of urine leakage. "As estrogen levels decline, vaginal and urinary tract muscles may weaken, making it more likely you'll have episodes of incontinence explains Diana Bitner, MD, an ob-gyn who specializes in menopause at Spectrum Health in Grand Rapids, Michigan. If you've put on weight, your odds of incontinence grow, thanks to increased pressure on your bladder and surrounding muscles.

Try this: Vaginal estrogen. You apply it—as either a prescription cream, suppository, or vaginal ring—to your genital area to replace declining estrogen in those tissues. "It will definitely ease urinary incontinence as well as symptoms like vaginal dryness, itching, and irritation says Bitner. Bonus: This boost of estrogen helps balance levels of vaginal bacteria, which in turn keeps vaginal pH (acidity) in line, reducing your risk of developing both yeast and urinary tract infections.

That's A Fact!

34

Pelvic floor exercise can help plug leaks: Participants in a Canadian clinical trial reduced their incidence of urinary incontinence by 75 percent after just 12 weekly sessions of physical therapy.

Not-So-Tenacious D

Called the sunshine vitamin because your skin synthesizes it after exposure to sunlight, vitamin D acts as a hormone to help maintain strong bones and modulate your immune system as well as your muscle and nerve function. Research suggests that vitamin D may also play a role in protecting cognition: In a University of Exeter study, adults 65 or older who were moderately deficient in vitamin D had a 53 percent higher risk of developing dementia; for the severely deficient, the risk rose to 125 percent. The potential to become deficient increases with age. "As you get older, your skin becomes less efficient in using the sun's rays to make vitamin D, so your body requires more explains Michal Melamed, MD, associate professor of medicine at Albert Einstein College of Medicine.

Try this: Consider a daily vitamin D supplement since you may not be able to get enough from food and UV exposure alone. While the Institute of Medicine recommends women in their 50s and 60s get 600 IUs daily, that's most likely not sufficient for everyone, says Melamed. In a small pilot study presented at the Society for Endocrinology's annual meeting last November, people who took 2,000 IUs daily for two weeks had lower blood

35

pressure, lower levels of the stress hormone cortisol, and better fitness performance than placebo takers. But don't exceed that amount. "Some research has linked high dosages to an increased risk of developing kidney stones stresses Melamed.

"There's a huge hormonal change that occurs around [the age of 50], particularly a decrease in estrogen and progesterone . "However, with every passing year at this age—and it's much more significant in the 60s and 70s—there's a decrease in the basal metabolic rate or the energy required to maintain body weight. There's also an increased need for protein in the diet to maintain the same muscle mass as a younger woman. Say you have 30 lbs of muscle at age 25. You'd need 0.8 g of protein/lb of body weight [to maintain it]. At age 50, women need [about] 1 g [of protein]. All these things are intertwined."

changes start gradually as women enter their 50s, when they also may become more sedentary or develop weight issues. "This can increase the risk of potentially chronic conditions such as hypertension, high cholesterol, and diabetes. She says the daily caloric intake of a woman in her 50s should be as follows:

• not very active: 1,600 kcal;

• moderately active: 1,800 kcal; and

• very active: 2,000 to 2,200 kcal.

In comparison, a 30-year-old woman needs 1,800 to 2,400 kcal per day.

Boning Up

In addition to hormonal and muscle mass decreases that accompany menopause, bone loss is another factor—although women can slow the rate of bone loss with weight-bearing exercise. "The more weight-bearing exercise you do, the better you're able to maintain bone density Gerbstadt explains. But bone mass will still decline due to hormonal decreases, which is why a woman's need for protein, calcium, and vitamin D increase at age 50 and beyond, she says.

Women can address their calcium and vitamin D requirements "100% through diet although supplements are an option, . These two minerals are connected in that vitamin D—actually the hormone calcitriol—is essential to calcium absorption, and vitamin D fortifies the immune system. It's currently recommended that women get 600 IUs of vitamin D per day. The goal for daily calcium intake is 1,200 mg per day.

"One cup of nonfat milk gives you 300 mg . Additional dairy sources of calcium include yogurt and cheese, though eating low-fat cottage cheese is best due to its lower fat content compared with other cheese varieties. Nondairy sources of calcium include fortified orange juice, soy milk, and breakfast cereal.

Finding Friendly Fats

Nutrient-rich, unsaturated fats, crucial to aging healthfully, can guard against coronary artery disease, heart attack, and stroke and protect the myelin coating of nerve fibers, allowing them to work properly. "Fat also keeps your skin supple and your body from drying out . "Basically, it's like putting lotion on your body but from the inside out."

Women over 50 can increase their omega-3 fatty acid intake from supplements or eating three servings per week of tuna, salmon, mackerel, or sardines. They also can get omega-3s from avocados, nuts, and oils such as olive, walnut, and sesame as well as from seeds, including sunflower, sesame, pumpkin, chia, and flaxseed. "[All these foods] have different proportions of omega-3s, -6s, and -9s. You actually need all of them in the correct ratio .

But even though these fats contain omega-3s, Sheth recommends clients keep their total fat intake to less than 30% of daily calories and reduce saturated fat to 10% of daily calories.

Pumping Up Protein

When it comes to protein, RDs should recommend clients aim for 5 to 6 oz on average per day. "Make sure they get some at breakfast and about 2 to 3 oz at lunch and dinner .

38

Preferred meat sources include lean beef, such as tenderloin, bison, venison, skinless chicken breast, and pork loin with the outer fat trimmed. "Think of using meat as a garnish, not the focus of the meal .

Low- and nonfat yogurt, especially Greek yogurt, is another great protein source. Soybeans, pinto or kidney beans, and lentils are other options. "Those are excellent sources of protein and fiber to help keep the LDL, or bad, cholesterol low . "That's bang for your buck!"

Clients also can eat liquid egg whites (egg substitute), which can enhance many meals, or simply eat regular eggs. "If they don't want too many yolks, [they can] make an omelet with two to four whites and only one yolk . "That adds practically no additional calories but a lot more protein."

Telltale Signs of Nutrient Deficiencies

Women in their 50s who aren't eating a healthful diet may experience symptoms of nutrient deficiencies, although they may be subtle, . They may feel sluggish and experience forgetfulness, fractures or frequent injuries, or bleeding gums. Eating a nutrient-dense diet, coupled with regular physical activity, can combat fatigue; vitamin B12 can help improve memory; calcium and vitamin D can enhance bone density; and vitamin C and iron can prevent bleeding gums, , who suggests clients speak with their doctor about getting their vitamin D and B12 levels checked and receiving hormone replacement therapy, which may relieve hot flashes and help protect against osteoporosis.

Another symptom that can easily be prevented by drinking enough water is dehydration. "As we get older, our thirst mechanism isn't as effective . Older clients may not be aware that they're dehydrated or thirsty. To prevent dehydration, Sheth recommends women keep a bottle or glass of water on their nightstand. The Mayo Clinic's Adequate Intake recommendation for women is 2.2 L, or 9 cups, of beverages per day.

Avoiding, Adding, and Replacing

Often, making small changes can result in a huge payoff. If clients are used to reaching for simple sugars in the form of cookies and baked goods for a snack, suggest they eat three servings of fresh fruit each day. If they enjoy the skin as well, they'll get more nutrients.

Moreover, women should choose whole grains whenever possible. Even if a bagel claims to be multigrain, that's not a whole grain flour. Go with oatmeal instead.

There's a need to stress the importance of fiber to promote bowel regularity, flush cholesterol from their system, lower the risk of heart disease, and keep weight in check. "When you have a lot of volume in your stomach, you don't feel the need to eat or snack as frequently. Women over 50 need to keep in mind that fiber needs water to swell up and go through their systems." So tell clients to aim for 25 to 30 g of fiber per day from whole grains, legumes, and vegetables.

And with regard to sodium intake, women aged 50 and older should get no more than 1,500 mg per day. "That's not much. "Just 1 tsp of salt has about 2,400 mg of sodium."

And for a treat, it is advisable eat just one piece of high-quality dark chocolate each day to promote heart health.

Shaking Up Mealtime

Nutritional drinks in liquid and powder form, such as Boost and Ensure, have been growing in popularity as nutritious and satisfying meal replacements. But are these convenient products really beneficial?

Women in their 50s and 60s may not feel satisfied after drinking a meal replacement product, which could lead to overeating and weight gain. But a woman in her 80s may need to supplement her diet with a nutritional drink since weight maintenance in later decades is a challenge due to lack of appetite,

Evaluating the consumption of meal replacement drinks with Women over 50 on a case-by-case basis. "If a client doesn't have the energy to assemble a meal, it's nice to have something ready-made she says. "It doesn't really take the place of a complete meal, but it's good to have as a backup."

It is necessary that clients read labels before purchasing these products. She says a good meal replacement will contain 280 to 300 kcal per serving, 25 to 30 g of carbohydrates, 5 g of fiber, and less than 20 g of sugar.

How It Affects Your Cells and Hormones
When you fast, several things happen in your body on the cellular and molecular level. For example, your body adjusts hormone levels to make stored body fat more accessible. Your cells also initiate important repair processes and change the expression of genes.

Here are some changes that occur in your body when you fast:

Human Growth Hormone (HGH): The levels of growth hormone skyrocket, increasing as much as 5-fold. This has benefits for fat loss and muscle gain, to name a few.
Insulin: Insulin sensitivity improves and levels of insulin drop dramatically. Lower insulin levels make stored body fat more accessible.

Cellular repair: When fasted, your cells initiate cellular repair processes. This includes autophagy, where cells digest and remove old and dysfunctional proteins that build up inside cells.

Gene expression: There are changes in the function of genes related to longevity and protection against disease.

These changes in hormone levels, cell function and gene expression are responsible for the health benefits of intermittent fasting.

When you fast, human growth hormone levels go up and insulin levels go down. Your body's cells also change the expression of genes and initiate important cellular repair processes.

A Very Powerful Weight Loss Tool

Weight loss is the most common reason for people to try intermittent fasting.

By making you eat fewer meals, intermittent fasting can lead to an automatic reduction in calorie intake. Additionally, intermittent fasting changes hormone levels to facilitate weight loss.

In addition to lowering insulin and increasing growth hormone levels, it increases the release of the fat burning hormone norepinephrine (noradrenaline).

43

Because of these changes in hormones, short-term fasting may increase your metabolic rate by 3.6–14%.

By helping you eat fewer and burn more calories, intermittent fasting causes weight loss by changing both sides of the calorie equation.

Studies show that intermittent fasting can be a very powerful weight loss tool.

A 2014 review study found that this eating pattern can cause 3–8% weight loss over 3–24 weeks, which is a significant amount, compared to most weight loss studies (1).

According to the same study, people also lost 4–7% of their waist circumference, indicating a significant loss of harmful belly fat that builds up around your organs and causes disease (1).

Another study showed that intermittent fasting causes less muscle loss than the more standard method of continuous calorie restriction (16).

However, keep in mind that the main reason for its success is that intermittent fasting helps you eat fewer calories overall. If you binge and eat massive amounts during your eating periods, you may not lose any weight at all.

Intermittent fasting may slightly boost metabolism while helping you eat fewer calories. It's a very effective way to lose weight and belly fat.

Health Benefits

Many studies have been done on intermittent fasting, in both animals and humans.

These studies have shown that it can have powerful benefits for weight control and the health of your body and brain. It may even help you live longer.

Though you cannot eat anything during your fasting period, you are allowed to drink zero-calorie drinks throughout the day. The most important of these drinks is plain water, which can keep hunger at bay while helping you stay hydrated.

Though certain coffees and teas are also allowed, you should try to limit them as much as possible. At most, you should be drinking only two cups of a caffeinated beverage during your fasting day.

You would also have to break your fast the right way. Some beginners make the mistake of eating unhealthy foods once they have completed a 24-hour fasting period. To prevent you from committing the same mistake, here is a list of foods that you may eat after fasting:

- Raw vegetable slices, such as fresh carrots, cucumber, broccoli, and celery
- Hard-boiled eggs
- Unsalted nuts, such as cashews and walnuts

Try to have these post-fast snacks ready before even going into a fast. Heading to the grocery store during or right after your finishing your fast would only cause you to buy more foods than you actually need. You might also be tempted to buy certain food products that look appealing but are not exactly healthy choices for you.

Health experts also recommend taking dietary supplements while you are engaged in intermittent fasting. Your options include multivitamins, fish oil, and other common supplements that you normally take while you are not on a fast.

In terms of beverages, you should stick to pure water, unsweetened tea, black coffee, and other zero-calorie beverages. There are several diet beverages out there that claims to be good for your health. Avoid them at all cost because they might contain harmful chemicals that could negatively affect your health.

In fact, even non-caloric artificial sweeteners, such as aspartame and stevia, are highly discouraged among people who are engaged in fasting. You should be giving your body a break from these chemicals, especially since you are putting more strain on your body while you are in a fast

Intermittent fasting is certainly not for everyone.

If you're underweight or have a history of eating disorders, you should not fast without consulting with a health professional first. In these cases, it can be downright harmful.

Should Women Fast?

There is some evidence that intermittent fasting may not be as beneficial for women as it is for men.

For example, one study showed that it improved insulin sensitivity in men, but worsened blood sugar control in women.

Though human studies on this topic are unavailable, studies in rats have found that intermittent fasting can make female rats emaciated, masculinized and infertile and cause them to miss cycles.

There are a number of anecdotal reports of women whose menstrual period stopped when they started doing IF and went back to normal when they resumed their previous eating pattern. For these reasons, women should be careful with intermittent fasting.

They should follow separate guidelines, like easing into the practice and stopping immediately if they have any problems like amenorrhea (absence of menstruation).

If you have issues with fertility and/or are trying to conceive, consider holding off on intermittent fasting for now. This eating pattern is likely also a bad idea if you're pregnant or breastfeeding.

People who are underweight or have a history of eating disorders should not fast. There is also some evidence that intermittent fasting may be harmful to some women.

Safety and Side Effects

Hunger is the main side effect of intermittent fasting. You may also feel weak and your brain may not perform as well as you're used to. This may only be temporary, as it can take some time for your body to adapt to the new meal schedule. If you have a medical condition, you should consult with your doctor before trying intermittent fasting.

This is particularly important if you:

Have diabetes.

Have problems with blood sugar regulation.

Have low blood pressure.

Take medications.

Are underweight.

Have a history of eating disorders.

Are a woman who is trying to conceive.

Are a woman with a history of amenorrhea.

Are pregnant or breastfeeding.

All that being said, intermittent fasting has an outstanding safety profile. There is nothing dangerous about not eating for a while if you're healthy and well-nourished overall.

The most common side effect of intermittent fasting is hunger. People with certain medical conditions should not fast without consulting with a doctor first.

HEALTHLINE CHALLENGES

Looking to cut back on sugar? I'll give you some sweet tips

Our Nutrition newsletter's 10 day sugar challenge guides you in bringing more awareness to the sugars in the foods you eat and gives you the tools you need to make healthier choices. Let's get started!

We're going to take two widely accepted healthy eating "rules" and turn them on their head:

RULE (1): You HAVE to eat first thing in the morning: Make sure you start off with a healthy breakfast, so you can get that metabolism firing first thing in the morning!

"Eat breakfast like a king, lunch like a prince, and dinner like a pauper."

There are even studies that show those that eat earlier in the day lose more weight than those who ate later in the day or skipped a meal.

RULE (2): Eat lots of small meals for weight loss. Make sure you eat six small meals throughout the day so your metabolism stays operating at maximum capacity all day long."

In other words, "eat breakfast and lots of small meals to lose weight and obtain optimal health." But what if there's science and research that shows SKIPPING BREAKFAST (the horror! blasphemy!) can help with optimum human performance, mental and physical health improvement, maximum muscle retention, and body fat loss? This cat is surprised at the evidence that fasting may be better than eating breakfast.

That's where an Intermittent Fasting Plan comes in. Intermittent fasting is not a diet, but rather a dieting pattern.
In simpler terms: it's making a conscious decision to skip certain meals on purpose.

By fasting and then feasting deliberately, intermittent fasting generally means that you consume your calories during a specific window of the day, and choose not to eat food for a larger window of time. There are a few different ways to take advantage of intermittent fasting, which I learned about from Martin over at LeanGains, a resource specifically built around fasted strength training:

What it is: Fasting for 16 hours and then only eating within a specific 8-hour window. For example, only eating from noon-8 PM, essentially skipping breakfast.

Some people only eat in a 6-hour window, or even a 4-hour window. This is "feasting" and "fasting" parts of your days and the most common form of Intermittent Fasting. It's also my preferred method (4 years running).

Two examples: The top means you are skipping breakfast, the bottom means you are skipping dinner each day:
This is an example of an intermittent fasting plan. Download our worksheet to create your own!
You can adjust this window to make it work for your life:
If you start eating at: 7AM, stop eating and start fasting at 3pm.
If you start eating at: 11AM, stop eating and start fasting at 7pm.
If you start eating at: 2PM, stop eating and start fasting at 10pm.
If you start eating at: 6PM, stop eating and start fasting at 2AM.

INTERMITTENT FASTING 24 HOUR PLAN
Skip two meals one day, where you take 24 hours off from eating. For example, eat on a normal schedule (finishing dinner at 8PM) and then you don't eat again until 8PM the following day.

With this plan, you eat your normal 3 meals per day, and then occasionally pick a day to skip breakfast and lunch the next day. If you can only do an 18 hour fast, or a 20 hour fast, or a 22 hour fast – that's okay! Adjust with different time frames and see how your body responds. Two examples: skipping breakfast and lunch one day of the week, and then another where you skip lunch and dinner one day, two days in a week. This shows another schedule you can try for your intermittent fasting plan.

Note: You can do this once a week, twice a week, or whatever works best for your life and situation. By the way, both those weekly charts above come from our free Intermittent Fasting Plan (with printable worksheets). Most people struggle with knowing exactly when to eat and when to stop eating, and actually sticking with it.

Those are the two most popular intermittent fasting plans, and the two we'll be focusing on, though there are many variations of both that you can modify for yourself.

Some people eat in a 4 hour window, others do 6 or 8.

Some people do 20 hour fasts or 24 hour fasts.

You'll need to experiment, adjust to work for your lifestyle and goals, and see how your body responds. Let's first get into the science here behind Intermittent Fasting and why you should consider it!

To guide on selecting the right fasting method for you, here is a rundown of the effective options that most people choose:

Fasting has been a practice throughout human evolution. Ancient hunter-gatherers didn't have supermarkets, refrigerators or food available year-round. Sometimes they couldn't find anything to eat. As a result, humans evolved to be able to function without food for extended periods of time. In fact, fasting from time to time is more natural than always eating 3–4 (or more) meals per day. Fasting is also often done for religious or spiritual reasons, including in Islam, Christianity, Judaism and Buddhism.

The level of dietary strictness also differs from method to another. Some methods do not allow the follower to consume anything except for water, while controlled fasts aim to only reduce your daily caloric intake.

To help you assess the potentials of intermittent fasting as the ideal fasting protocol for you, here are its pros over the other methods discussed in this book.

- You are free to adjust your fasting schedule according to your preferences.

  The day and timing of your fasting does not matter as long as you do it on a weekly basis. Some people prefer doing intermittent fasting during the weekends, while some have an easier time doing it on weekdays.

  Pick the best day and time for you so that you would be more successful in sticking with intermittent fasting. Just avoid drawing it beyond the suggested 24-hour fasting period to prevent the occurrence of any health complications.

- You may use your fasting day to engage in fulfilling and more productive activities.
  Taking a break from eating, even for just a day, would give you more opportunities to pursue other worthwhile activities. For one day per week, you are free from having to prepare and cook your meals, or think about where you are going to eat.

- You can save more money from your weekly budget allocation for food.
  Because you are not going to eat during certain times and days of the week, you would be able to reduce your weekly grocery bill.
  It is also important for you to recognize the downsides of intermittent fasting before making a decision. For your guidance, here are the known cons of this fasting method.

- The 24-hour duration may be too difficult to observe, especially among beginners.
  If you have not experienced fasting before, you are likely going to feel disoriented by the common side-effects of intermittent fasting, such as having low energy for a significant portion of your fasting day. Some people also experience a hard time in staving off their hunger.

- It may take you a while before you can get accustomed to the negative effects of intermittent fasting on your body.

  You can eventually overcome these challenges, provided that you would practice proper intermittent fasting on a regular basis.

  Some experts suggest taking baby steps before taking on the full 24-hour duration of this method. At the very least, you should aim to fast for 22 hours in order to reap the benefits of intermittent fasting.

- Weight loss: As mentioned above, intermittent fasting can help you lose weight and belly fat, without having to consciously restrict calories.

- Insulin resistance: Intermittent fasting can reduce insulin resistance, lowering blood sugar by 3–6% and fasting insulin levels by 20–31%, which should protect against type 2 diabetes.

- Inflammation: Some studies show reductions in markers of inflammation, a key driver of many chronic diseases.

- Heart health: Intermittent fasting may reduce "bad" LDL cholesterol, blood triglycerides, inflammatory markers, blood sugar and insulin resistance — all risk factors for heart disease.

- Cancer: Animal studies suggest that intermittent fasting may prevent cancer.

- Brain health: Intermittent fasting increases the brain hormone BDNF and may aid the growth of new nerve cells. It may also protect against Alzheimer's disease.

- Anti-aging: Intermittent fasting can extend lifespan in rats. Studies showed that fasted rats lived 36–83% longer.
- Keep in mind that research is still in its early stages. Many of the studies were small, short-term or conducted in animals. Many questions have yet to be answered in higher quality human studies.

- Intermittent fasting can have many benefits for your body and brain. It can cause weight loss and may reduce your risk of type 2 diabetes, heart disease and cancer. It may also help you live longer.

- Makes Your Healthy Lifestyle Simpler
- Eating healthy is simple, but it can be incredibly hard to maintain.
- One of the main obstacles is all the work required to plan for and cook healthy meals.

- Intermittent fasting can make things easier, as you don't need to plan, cook or clean up after as many meals as before.
- For this reason, intermittent fasting is very popular among the life-hacking crowd, as it improves your health while simplifying your life at the same time.

- One of the major benefits of intermittent fasting is that it makes healthy eating simpler. There are fewer meals you need to prepare, cook and clean up after.

(1) Don't freak out! Stop wondering: "can I fast 15 hours instead of 16?" or "what if I eat an apple during my fasted period, will that ruin everything?" Relax. Your body is a complex piece of machinery and learns to adapt. Everything is not as cut and dry as you think.

If you want to eat breakfast one day but not another, that's okay. If you are going for optimal aesthetic or athletic performance, I can see the need to be more rigid in your discipline, but otherwise...freaking chill out and don't stress over minutiae!

This leopard knows that you'll be fine while doing intermittent fasting, just try it out and you'll be fine.
Don't let perfect be the enemy of good when it comes to your intermittent fasting plan.

(2) Consider fasted walks in the morning. I found these to be very helpful in reducing body fat, and also gave my day a great start to clear my mind and prepare for the day.

Simply wake up and go for a mile walk. Maybe you could even start walking to Mordor?

(3) Listen to your body during your strength training workouts. If you get light headed, make sure you are consuming enough water.

If you notice a significant drop in performance, make sure you are eating enough calories (especially fats and protein) during your feasting window.

And if you feel severely "off," pause your workout. Give yourself permission to EASE into intermittent fasting and fasted workouts. This is especially true if you are an endurance athlete.

(4) Expect funny looks if you spend a lot of mornings with breakfast eaters.

A few weeks back I had a number of friends staying with me, and they were all completely dumbfounded when I told them I didn't eat breakfast anymore.

I tried to explain it to them but received a bunch of blank stares. Breakfast has become so enGRAINed (zing!) in our culture that NOT eating it sounds crazy.

You will get weird looks from those around you...embrace it. I still go to brunch or sit with friends, I just drink black coffee and enjoy a conversation.

(5) Stay busy. If you are just sitting around thinking about how hungry you are, you'll be more likely to struggle with this. For that reason, I time my fasting periods for maximum efficiency and minimal discomfort:

My first few hours of fasting come after consuming a MONSTER dinner, where the last thing I want to think about is eating.
When I'm sleeping: 8 of my 16 hours are occupied by sleeping. Tough to feel hungry when I'm dreaming about becoming a Jedi.
When I'm busy: After waking up, 12 hours of my fasting is already done. I spend three hours doing my best work (while drinking a cup of black coffee), and then comes my final hour of fasting: training.

(6) Zero-calorie beverages are okay. I drink green tea in the morning for my caffeine kick while writing. If you want to drink water, black coffee, or tea during your fasted period, that's okay. Remember, don't overthink it – keep things simple! Dr. Rhonda Patrick over at FoundMyFitness believes that a fast should stop at the first consumption of anything other than water, so experiment yourself and see how your body responds. If you want to put milk in your coffee, or drink diet soda occasionally while fasting, I'm not going to stop you. Remember, we're going for consistency and habit-building here – if milk or cream in your coffee makes life worth living, don't deprive yourself.

There are MUCH bigger fish to fry with regards to getting healthy than a few calories here and there during a fast. 80% adherence that you stick with for a year is better than 100% adherence that you abandon after a month because it was too restrictive.

If you're trying to get to a minimum bodyfat percentage, you'll need to be more strict – until then, however, do what allows you to stay compliant!

(7) Track your results, listen to your body:

Concerned about losing muscle mass? Keep track of your strength training routines and see if you are getting stronger.
Buy a cheap set of body fat calipers and keep track of your body fat composition.
Track your calories, and see how your body changes when eating the same amount of food, but condensed into a certain window.
Everybody will react to an Intermittent Fasting Plan differently; I can't tell you how your body will react. It's up to you to listen to your body and see how making these adjustments change your body.

(8) Don't expect miracles. Yes, Intermittent Fasting can potentially help you lose weight, increase insulin sensitivity and growth hormone secretion (all good things), but it is only ONE

64

factor in hundreds that will determine your body composition and overall health. Don't expect to drop to 8% body fat and get ripped just by skipping breakfast.

Getting Started with Intermittent Fasting: Next Steps
Don't overthink intermittent fasting. Relax, try it, and see how you feel!
Intermittent fasting can potentially have some very positive benefits for somebody trying to lose weight or gain lean body mass.

Men and women will tend to have different results, just like each individual person will have different results. The ONLY way to find out is through a conversation with your doctor and self-experimentation. There are multiple ways to "do" an Intermittent Fasting Plan: Fast and feast regularly: Fast for a certain number of hours, then consume all calories within a certain number of hours.

Eat normally, then fast 1-2x a week: Consume your normal meals every day, then pick one or two days a week where you fast for 24 hours. Eat your last meal Sunday night, and then don't eat again until dinner the following day.
Fast occasionally: probably the easiest method for the person who wants to do the least amount of work. Simply skip a meal

whenever it's convenient. On the road? Skip breakfast. Busy day at work? Skip lunch. Eat poorly all day Saturday? Make your first meal of the day dinner on Sunday.

After that, get started! Take photos, step on the scale, and track your progress for the next month.

See how your body responds.

See how your physique changes. See how your workouts change.

And then decide if it's something you want to keep doing!

IS IF EFFECTIVE FOR WEIGHT LOSS?

Studies found that the amount of weight lost following an alternate day fast was equal to that lost via a typical low calorie weight loss plan. However, as the description reveals, this is a challenging fasting pattern, and side effects reported included serious hunger pangs and decreased concentration on the fasting days. Also, some studies revealed that people ate more than usual on non-fasting days. Thus, they did not restrict enough calories to promote weight loss. Plus, the long-term effects on your health of this eating pattern are not yet known. More research is needed on alternative day fasting as an approach to weight loss.

As its name suggest, the general principle behind this method is going on a fast every other day. In its most basic form, you would be allowed to drink only zero-calorie drinks during your fasting days.

Some forms, however, permit the consumption of meals that do not exceed the 500-calorie limit. Whichever the case may be, as long as you are fasting every other day, then you are engaging in the alternate-day fasting method.

Here are the pros of choosing this strategy:

- You only have to fast half of the time.

- Compared to other fasting methods that must be done on a daily basis in order to have an impact on your health, the mechanics of the alternate-fasting enables you to live and eat as you normally do on your off-days.
- Remember to keep things on the healthy side, however, because reverting back to processed food and sugary beverages during your break from fasting would be detrimental to the overall success of this method.

- It is more effective at preserving your muscle mass compared to the other fasting methods.

- Normally, the rate of fat-burning within your body is directly correlated to the loss of muscle mass. As such, those who are hoping to obtain leaner muscles through a fast may find it hard to maintain the muscle tissues that they have developed through exercising.
- On the other hand, studies show that those who the alternate-day fasting manage to maintain their muscle mass even though they have lost more body fat than those who belong to other test groups. Therefore, if you aiming to build your muscles while you are losing your excess weight, then the most appropriate method for you may be the alternate-day fasting.

- It can trigger the process of autophagy.

68

- Autophagy plays a critical role in removing the damaged components from your cells and organ systems. Through this process, you would be able to significantly lessen your chances of developing serious chronic illnesses, such as cancer, cardiovascular diseases, and various types of bodily infections.

- The problem is that it does not automatically occur, unless it is triggered. One way to do so is by adapting the alternate-day fasting. Researchers have found out that through this method, you would be able to reduce the damage in your body caused by oxidation. As a result, this could also increase your longevity in the process of cleansing your body from within.

- To even things out, here are the cons of the alternate-day fasting that you have to consider:

- Due to the fasting schedule of this method, it may take a while before you can get used to being in a fasted state.

- Some people consider the lack of continuity per day as the reason for their slow adjustment towards the changes in their life caused by fasting. This pertains more on the negative side-effects such as more frequent hunger pangs, lightheadedness, and low energy levels.

- Since you only have to undergo fasting every other day, your body and mind may not become acclimatized to fasting within the expected one to two-week adjustment period.

- The weight loss effects of alternate-day fasting may not be as quick as the other fasting methods.

69

- Again, since you are not restricting your calorie intake during your off-days, you might notice that you are not shedding off your excess weight, especially during the first few times you have implemented this method.
- As verified by multiple studies, the amount of body fat that you may lose through fasting tends to be compounded by the water weight that you also lose during a fast. This water weight, unlike body fat, can be easily regained whenever you consume foods without exercising at all.
- To keep you on track with your weight loss goals while following the alternate-day fasting, you should increase your exercise during your off-days. This would enable you to exert control over the possibility of regaining your water weight.
- You should also be mindful of the meal restrictions for alternate-day fasting.

- If you are following a sub-form of this method where you are allowed to eat, you should eat meals and snacks that would not total up to more than 500 calories per day.

- Therefore, you should go for highly nutritious yet filling foods, such as organic vegetables, leans meats, and fish.

- In order to feel full despite the lower calories, you should include more soup into your meal plan. Salads with generous helpings of lean meat may also be a good option for you, especially during your off-days.

- For drinks, you should stick to low-calorie or zero-calorie beverages, such as water, herbal tea, and black coffee.

EXERCISES FOR WOMEN OVER 50 AND BEYOND

According to the American Council on Exercise, your resting metabolic rate, aka your body's ability to burn calories while doing nothing, decreases by about one to two percent per decade due to muscle mass loss and increased fat mass. To add insult to pudge-boosting injury, your diets often don't change enough to account for this metabolic slow-down, meaning weight can creep up slowly but surely with every birthday.

"There are a number of roadblocks people in their 50s will face when trying to lose weight," says Brian Durbin, a NSCA-certified strength and conditioning specialist and personal trainer. "But once you know what they are—and how to work around them—it's easy to be successful at dropping pounds."

While it's not impossible to lose weight after 50, the methods you used in your 30s or 40s are not going to work the same way. Follow these tips to help you drop the pounds and keep them off for good:

71

It's never a good idea to create a weight-loss plan for yourself without speaking to your physician first—especially if you have any preexisting health conditions. "Before you get started, it helps to fully understand your current state of health before beginning any diet or exercise plan," advises Dr. Petre.

Be clear with your doctor what you hope to achieve, and ask for suggestions regarding diet and exercise. Your doc may even be able to recommend a physical therapist or personal trainer for you.

Get your hormones checked

As we age, progesterone, testosterone, and other hormones decline, which sets the body up for storing fat instead of losing weight, says Jennifer Burns, NMD, a naturopathic physician in Phoenix. "Simply getting your thyroid, adrenal glands, and other hormone levels checked—and then taking the appropriate steps to bring them back into balance—can go a long way toward helping people in their 50s lose weight," says Burns.

Tami Meraglia, MD, author of The Hormone Secret: Discover Effortless Weight Loss and Renewed Energy in Just 30 Days, agrees, adding that she believes the hormone to focus on is testosterone—especially for women over 50 who are trying to get fit. "There is ample discussion in the medical community about the effects of estrogen loss, but few people are aware of the importance of sufficient testosterone levels, which can help a woman slim down," says Dr. Meraglia. In fact, research shows that balanced testosterone levels reduce blood glucose levels, which may help promote weight loss and shrink stubborn belly fat.

Set realistic goals

Declaring that you're going to lose 20 pounds in one month is unrealistic, not to mention unhealthy. "Be honest with yourself. How do you feel? How healthy are you? Making life changes takes courage and mental fortitude," says Dr. Petre. Be realistic—and break up big goals into smaller, more achievable ones. Focusing on how you're feeling and the positive changes you're making to your lifestyle, instead of the number on the scale, will help you stay motivated to reach your goals. "Triumphs make your courage grow," she adds. "Small achievements amount to large goals achieved."

Hire a dietitian

If you're not sure which diet works best for your lifestyle, talking to a dietitian can help you identify the right eating plan for you. Whether you're considering the Flexitarian Diet, intermittent fasting, or even keto, a dietitian can break down the pros and cons of each plan and help you choose one that fits your nutritional needs and goals. Consulting an RD will also give you ideas on how to resolve road blocks that may get in the way of your weight-loss goals, like emotional/stress eating, food sensitivities, nutritional deficiencies, meal boredom, etc.

Follow a structured plan

If you want to succeed in losing weight, following a structured plan can help, says Dr. Petre. "Instead of trying and failing at yet another yo-yo diet this year, it's time to get serious about your health by following a trusted program," she suggests. She explains that medically supervised programs have a success rate for weight loss of more than 75 percent. "It has been proven that individual support programs can encourage a significant change in behavior and reinforce long-term success," she adds. Diet programs that include weekly visits can also provide accountability and continued support to keep the momentum going.

The best diets for weight loss 2019 include the Mediterranean Diet, the DASH Diet, and the MIND diet. These diets have been proven to support weight loss, while also improving your health and reducing your risk for heart disease, diabetes, and Alzheimer's, among other health conditions.

Embrace strength training

If you find it tough to make it to the gym at all, let alone brave a weight room filled with buff 20-somethings, here's a little motivation: Once you hit 50, you've got about 20 percent less muscle mass than you did when you were 20. And because muscle is metabolically active, muscle loss equals a slower metabolism. That makes you much more likely to put on (and hold on to) extra pounds, says Durbin. "The good news is you can turn all of this around with a well-structured weight-training routine," he says. "That can increase your muscle mass and help you regain the ability to lose weight like you were able to 20 years ago," he says. Aim to lift weights at least twice a week, whether you use free weights, machines or do bodyweight exercises. It doesn't hurt to lift every day—just make sure to work different muscle groups or train differently each day.

Choose activities that are easy on the joints

Janna Lowell, a Los Angeles–based personal trainer, says she gets the best results among her 50-somethings when she has them do some cross training in the pool. Tired joints can keep this population from getting a great workout, she says, and aches and pains can turn some people off exercise completely. "Water exercise is easy on the joints and can boost range of motion as well," says Lowell. "Even better, caloric expenditure is about 30 percent greater in the water than on land due to the resistance water creates." No pool? No problem. Walking is another great, low-impact cardiovascular exercise, as are cycling, kayaking, yoga, and dancing.

Make the most out of every workout

Just because your joints are a little achier than they used to be doesn't give you an excuse to phone in your workouts. Alex Allred, a former national and professional athlete turned personal trainer, says this is one of her biggest pet peeves among 50-year-olds. "Far too many people think that just because they showed up, they're working out," says Allred. "But really, you need to be focused on what you're doing and pushing yourself hard enough to break a sweat or at least complete the full range of motion of a certain exercise." Not sure if you're doing a move properly? Ask! "I wish more people would flag down a trainer and ask, 'Am I doing this correctly?' " says Allred. It can make the difference between making the most of your exercise time to lose weight and wasting your time and injuring yourself.

See a physical therapist

The advice to consult your doctor before starting any new exercise regimen is great, but Samira Shuruk, an ACE-certified personal trainer, suggests taking this advice a step further: Make an appointment with a physical therapist—particularly if an aching back, knee, or other body part has kept you from working out on a regular basis. "After 50, many people have sustained injuries and don't know what their activity options are," says Shuruk. "This makes it tough to exercise in ways we used to, and getting advice from a professional can truly help." Physical therapy can also help you rehabilitate an old injury or ease joint and muscle pain, setting you up for pain-free workouts.

Overhaul your diet

Remember that metabolic slow-down? It can mean that you're burning about 250 fewer calories each day. If you continue to eat like you're in your 30s—and don't increase your exercise—you'll gain weight, plain and simple, says Katie Ferraro, RD, a dietitian and assistant clinical professor of nutrition at the University of California–San Francisco School of Nursing. "To lose weight when you get older, you have to eat fewer calories," says Ferraro. Eliminating the junk food in your diet and replacing them with loads of fruits, vegetables, whole grains, and lean proteins can make cutting calories painless.

Change how and when you eat

It's not just what you eat, but how you eat that matters in your 50s, claims Anthony Dissen, MA, RDN, Vice President of Nutrition at WellStart Health. He suggests focusing on fullness, not portion control, when you are planning your meals. "If our stomachs aren't full, we don't feel full, and we'll stay hungry," he points out. "When it comes to healthy weight loss and management, we want to strike that important balance between

77

eating until we feel full and satisfied while still decreasing our overall calorie intake."

Also, stay away from fad diets. "No crazy fasts, cleanses, cutting out fats, or complex carbohydrates or proteins," adds Jillian Michaels, health and wellness expert and author of The 6 Keys: Unlock Your Genetic Potential for Ageless Strength, Health and Beauty.

Get your stress in check

This decade can be prime time for stress, says Durbin. "The average 50-year-old has many more responsibilities than their younger peers. They're often in their prime income-generating years, which means extra responsibilities at work. They may also have kids who are going to college—a financial burden—or have aging parents who they're helping to care for." The result? Emotional eating and a schedule that seems too jam-packed for regular exercise sessions. The solution: Schedule your workouts like they're doctor's appointments, says Durbin. Sticking to a consistent routine can not only help ease stress, but also help people stay on track with their diets. After all, who wants to ruin the benefits of a tough sweat session by eating a donut?

Get your sleep

Getting 7 to 8 hours of sleep every night is key, maintains Michaels. In addition to leaving you feeling rested, Dr. Petre adds that the two hormones that regulate appetite—leptin and ghrelin—go into overdrive without it. "This can trigger excessive hunger and lead to poor food choices and weight gain at any age," she says.

Be mindful... and meditate

It's important to practice mindfulness, especially when you're eating. Dr. Dissen explains that most people have more control over their time and schedules during their 50s than ever before, due to decreased responsibilities with work and family, and they should take advantage of it. "The more we try to multi-task while we eat, the more likely we are to overeat and not feel as satisfied by the meal or snack we've just eaten," he explains. "By simply taking a breath and treating our mealtime as special, it allows us to really taste our food and notice its flavors, textures, and tastes."

Mindfulness can aid in stress relief, which is important because many people eat or put off exercise when they are anxious. Michaels suggests practicing five to 10 minutes of meditation daily to maintain your brain's neuroplasticity and stress management.

Practice self-care

Practicing self-care, whether it's treating yourself to manicure or taking a mental health day from work, shouldn't be looked at as a luxury. The smallest gestures can make a big difference in reducing overall stress, which can make a big impact on your weight loss. When you show yourself a little more love, you can turn your energy into doing things that support your goals, like eating healthy, exercising, and meditating. Not sure how to start a self-care routine? First ask yourself why you need more time to take care of yourself. Are you working too many late hours at the office? Do you feel burned out and wish you could be calmer? Once you figure out why you need to make some more time for yourself, it can help you decide what will be a good activity or routine for you.

BREAKFAST RECIPES

Priscilla's Vegetable Chowder

This is the perfect soup to warm up with on a cold fall or winter day. Serve it in a bread bowl to make it extra special.

Total Time

Prep: 25 min. Cook: 30 min.

Makes

12 servings (3 quarts)

Ingredients

3 cups diced peeled potatoes

2-1/2 cups broccoli florets

1 cup chopped onion

1 cup grated carrots

2 celery ribs, diced

4 teaspoons chicken bouillon granules

3 cups water

3/4 cup butter, cubed

3/4 cup all-purpose flour

4 cups whole milk

1 teaspoon salt

1/4 teaspoon pepper

1 cup cubed fully cooked ham

1 cup Kerrygold shredded cheddar cheese

Directions

In a Dutch oven, combine the potatoes, broccoli, onion, carrots, celery, bouillon and water; simmer for 20 minutes or until vegetables are tender.

In a large saucepan, melt butter; stir in flour. Cook and stir over medium heat for 2 minutes. Whisk in the milk, salt and pepper. Bring to a boil; cook and stir for 2 minutes or until thickened. Add to vegetable mixture with the ham; simmer 10 minutes or until heated through. Stir in cheese just until melted.

Nutrition Facts

1 cup: 281 calories, 18g fat (11g saturated fat), 58mg cholesterol, 853mg sodium, 22g carbohydrate (6g sugars, 2g fiber), 9g protein.

Tomato Pepper Bisque

Roasting tomatoes and vegetables concentrates their flavor iving this bisque a full-bodied taste without the use of cream.

Prep Time 15 minutes

Cook Time 20 minutes

Serving 4 people

INGREDIENTS

5 large tomatoes quartered

1 medium red bell pepper seeded and quartered

2 large yellow onions quartered

4 cloves garlic peeled

2 1/2 cups low sodium vegetable broth or homemade broth, or water

1/2 cup unsweetened non-dairy milk (or homemade)

1/2 tsp paprika

sea salt and pepper to taste

INSTRUCTIONS

Preheat oven to 400 degrees F. Line a large baking sheet with parchment paper and spread the tomatoes, onions and peppers onto it. Sprinkle with salt, pepper and paprika.

Bake in the oven for about 5 minutes and then add the garlic cloves. Continue to roast the vegetables until they soften and start to caramelize, about 15 minutes, stirring about halfway through. Check to see if they're browning.

Put the vegetables into a large soup pot and add the vegetable broth. Use an immersion blender to process until smooth and then heat through. Or if you'd like to use a blender, add the tomatoes to it after roasting with enough broth to blend. Then add the blended tomatoes to the pot with the rest of the broth and heat through.

Add 1/2 cup of unsweetened non-dairy milk and stir to combine. Taste and add up to 1/2 cup more, if needed. Season with salt, pepper, and more paprika.

NUTRITION/NOTES

Amount Per Serving

Calories 114

Total Fat 2g3%

Total Carbohydrates 22g7%

Dietary Fiber 5.8g23%

Sugars 12.3g

Calcium7%

Iron9%

Instant Pot White Bean Soup with Garlic, Mushrooms and Farro

This makes an easy, delicious and super nutritious meal. Throw everything into the post (except the toppings and tomatoes) and cook on high and it'll be ready in less than 30 minutes.

Prep Time 20 minutes

Cook Time 22 minutes

Serving Size 8 people

1 1/2 cups

INGREDIENTS

1 1/2 cups dry cannellini beans rinsed and picked over for small stones or debris

1 cup farro

½ large onion chopped

2 8 oz containers mushrooms sliced

8 cloves garlic finely chopped

1/2 jalapeño pepper seeds removed and finely chopped

2 Tbl thai red curry paste or more to your liking. This isn't very hot.

1 shallot finely chopped

1 Tbl Braggs Liquid Aminos (optional)

10 cups homemade vegetable broth or low-salt store-bought to the fill line on a 6 quart Instant Pot (10 cups)

1 14.5 oz can diced tomatoes

Salt and Pepper to taste

Garnish

cilantro chopped

scallions chopped

dollop unsweetened plain yogurt optional

Mushroom Bean Soup

INSTRUCTIONS

Add all of the ingredients except the tomatoes, cilantro, and scallions in the Instant Pot

On "manual," setting and high pressure, cook for 22 minutes. If the beans are soft enough, turn on the Instant Pot again for another 5-7 minutes.

Quick release the press pressure and let sit for another 10-15 minutes on "Keep Warm" setting.

Stir in the diced tomatoes. Add salt and pepper to taste.

Serve topped with lots of cilantro and scallions. Add a dollop of yogurt if it suits your fancy.

NUTRITION/NOTES

 Amount Per Serving

Calories 297

Total Fat 1.4g2%

Total Carbohydrates 54g18%

Dietary Fiber 14.1g56%

Sugars 7.8g

Protein 17.5g35%

Calcium12%

Iron16%

How to Make Easy Plant-Based Vegetable Broth

Flavor your soups and saute vegetables with this easy low salt home plant-based vegetable broth made from your veggie scraps or fresh produce. Remember that you can mix up the combination by adding or leaving out any of the ingredients listed or use what you have on hand.

Prep Time 15 minutes

Cook Time 30 minutes

Serving Size 10 cups

INGREDIENTS

1 large onion (you can leave the skin on which adds color)

5 stalks celery chopped into large chunks

3 large carrots you don't need to peel them

1/3 head broccoli or other vegetable broken into chunks

4 cloves garlic with skin on

3 cups greens rough chopped

2 tomatoes chopped into large chunks

1/2 bunch parsley

4 oz mushrooms cut in half

2 bay leaves

1 tsp whole black peppercorns

½ tsp sea salt (optional)

10 cups water

Vegetable Broth

INSTRUCTIONS

Instant Pot INSTRUCTIONSs:

Chop the vegetables into large chunks.

Place all ingredients in the Instant Pot along with the water. Close lid and pressure cook on high pressure for 15 minutes. Natural release for 15 minutes and then turn the venting knob to the venting position to release the remaining pressure. Open the lid carefully.

Strain the broth through a large colander into a bowl to remove the larger pieces and then through a fine-mesh strainer to remove the last bits.

Keep in an air-tight container(s) or for smaller quantities, freeze in ice cube trays. Allow to cool and then refrigerate.

Stove Top Directions

Chop the vegetables into large chunks.

In a large pot over medium high heat, sauté the onions until fragrant (about 2 minutes). Add the garlic and sea salt and cook another 30 seconds.

Add the rest of the ingredients into the pot along with the water and bring to a boil. Gently stir to combine.

Simmer covered on low heat for about 1 hour. The longer you simmer it, the more concentrated it will be.

Strain the broth through a large colander to remove the larger pieces and then through a fine-mesh strainer to remove the rest.

Keep in an air-tight container(s) or for smaller quantities, freeze in ice cube trays. Allow to cool and then refrigerate.

NUTRITION/NOTES

does not include added salt

Nutrition Facts

How to Make Easy Plant-Based Vegetable Broth

Amount Per Serving

Calories 46Calories from Fat 4

Total Fat 0.4g1%

Saturated Fat 0.1g1%

Sodium 62.6mg3%

Total Carbohydrates 9.6g3%

Dietary Fiber 3.2g13%

Sugars 3.9g

Protein 2.6g5%

Vitamin A20%

Vitamin C68%

Calcium8%

Iron6%

This quick soup feels extra cozy with lots of lentils and a touch of smoky, bacony goodness. You might want to cook up extra.

Total Time
Prep: 15 min. Cook: 30 min.

Makes
8 servings (2 quarts)

Ingredients

4 bacon strips, chopped

6 medium carrots, chopped

2 small onions, diced

2 tablespoons tomato paste

2 garlic cloves, minced

1 teaspoon minced fresh thyme

1/2 teaspoon pepper

5 cups chicken stock

1 cup dry white wine or additional chicken stock

2 cans (15 to 16 ounces each) butter beans, rinsed and drained

9g of lentils, rinsed and drained

Fresh thyme sprigs, optional

Directions

In a Dutch oven, cook bacon over medium heat until crisp, stirring occasionally. Remove with a slotted spoon; drain on paper towels. Cook and stir carrots and onions in bacon dripping until crisp-tender, 3-4 minutes. Add tomato paste, garlic, thyme and pepper; cook 1 minute longer.

Add stock and wine; increase heat to medium-high. Cook 2 minutes, stirring to loosen browned bits from pan. Stir in butter beans, lentils and bacon. Bring to a boil. Reduce heat; simmer, covered, 5 minutes. Uncover; continue simmering until vegetables are tender, 15-20 minutes. Garnish with thyme sprigs, if desired.

Test Kitchen tips

Top with a dollop of sour cream for a cool flavor contrast.

Butter bean or lima bean, it's pretty much the same thing—although butter bean sounds a little more appealing to us.

Nutrition Facts

1 cup: 252 calories, 6g fat (2g saturated fat), 9mg cholesterol, 793mg sodium, 38g carbohydrate (7g sugars, 13g fiber), 17g protein. Diabetic Exchanges: 2-1/2 starch, 1 medium-fat meat.

Creamy Curried Cauliflower Soup

This is absolutely easy to make. It's warm and comforting while providing a great burst of plant-based nutrition with cauliflower, yams, red peppers and garbanzo beans for a little protein.

Prep Time 20 minutes

Cook Time 45 minutes

Serving Size 5 people

INGREDIENTS

1/2 lb potatoes peeled and cut into 1 1/2″ pieces

1/2 lb yams peeled and cut into 1 1/2″ pieces

1 large head of cauliflower cut into about 1 1/2″ pieces

1 1/2 cups sliced carrots (3 medium)

3/4 cup red bell pepper coarsely chopped, (1 medium)

1/2 cup chopped onion

Half cup cooked garbanzo beans rinsed and drained

3 tsp curry powder

2 tsp fresh ginger grated

1/2 tsp sea salt

1/8 tsp crushed red pepper

4 cups homemade vegetable broth or low sodium brand

1 14 cup of coconut milk

INSTRUCTIONS

Combine potatoes, cauliflower, carrots, sweet pepper, onion, and beans in a large pot over medium heat.

Sprinkle curry powder, ginger, crushed red pepper and salt over vegetables and beans. Pour broth over all.

Bring to a boil, cover and cook on low-heat for about 45 minutes or until vegetables are tender.

Stir in coconut milk and heat through. Note: If using a slow cooker, set on high for 4 hours or low for 8.

NUTRITION

Amount Per Serving

Calories 274

Total Fat 6.7g10%

Total Carbohydrates 47.3g16%

Dietary Fiber 12.5g50%

Sugars 11g

Protein 9.2g18%

Calcium11%

Iron13%

Spring Asparagus, Pea, Zucchini Soup with Pesto

This spring green soup is a delicate delight and a flavor bust with the addition of pesto. A quick and easy recipe that's great for guests or a weeknight meal.

Prep Time 15 minutes

Cook Time 15 minutes

Servings: 6 people

INGREDIENTS

1 bunch asparagus

1 cup English peas

3 medium zucchini sliced

1 medium onion chopped

2 cloves garlic chopped

5 cups low sodium vegetable broth , Trader Joe's (or 5 cups homemade)

1 coconut milk ,Trader Joe's

OR 1 tsp coconut extract mixed with 1 1/2 cups non-dairy milk

1/2 lemon juiced

1 teaspoon sea salt

1/4 teaspoon pepper

Pesto

1 1/2 cup fresh basil leaves tightly packed

1/2 cup parsley tightly packed

3 cloves garlic

1 Tbl light miso white or red

3 Tbl nutritional yeast

1/8 cup Pine nuts

3 Tbl fresh lemon juice

sea salt and pepper to taste

INSTRUCTIONS

In a large soup pot over medium heat, add the onion and garlic to about 1/4 cup water and sauté until fragrant, about 1 minute.

To prepare the asparagus, chop off the rough ends, then cut into 1" pieces. Add to the pot along with the zucchini, peas, vegetable broth and coconut milk (or coconut extract). Cover and simmer for about 25 minutes, or until the asparagus is tender.

Once the asparagus is tender, add the lemon juice, and salt and pepper. Blend in a high-speed blender in batches until smooth and creamy.

Transfer back to the soup pot until ready to serve. Ladle soup into bowls and garnish with a dollop of pesto.

Nutrition Facts

Amount Per Serving

Calories 220

Total Fat 5.5g8%

Total Carbohydrates 28.5g10%

Dietary Fiber 10.4g42%

Sugars 4.8g

Protein 17.1g34%

Calcium6%

Iron25%

Mary's Vegetable Soup with Farro

This Mary's Vegetable Soup recipe is chock-full of nutrient-dense vegetable and includes creamy cannellini beans, kale, Napa cabbage, and more. If you haven't tried farro, it's a wonderful substitute for rice with a chewy bite that's whole grain.

Prep Time 20 minutes

Cook Time 30 minutes

Servings 12 people

1 1/2 cups or 1 bowl

INGREDIENTS

2 1/2 boxes low sodium vegetable broth (or 10 cups homemade)

1 bunch napa cabbage sliced

2 inches leeks cut in half and then ¼" slices

1 1/2 cups potatoes chopped

1 onion chopped

3 carrots chopped

4 stalks celery chopped

2 cup kale and/or spinach, fresh or frozen, chopped

4 cloves garlic minced

3 cups of cooked cannellini beans with liquid

2 cooked sweet corn with liquid

2 cans diced tomatoes with liquid

1 cup farro

1 tsp sea salt

1/2 tsp ground pepper

1 Tbl fresh thyme

1 1/2 tsp dried tarragon

1 tsp dried coriander

½ tsp celery seed

½ tsp turmeric

INSTRUCTIONS

In a large stockpot, sauté leeks, onion, celery, carrots, potatoes, garlic in about 1/4 cup vegetable broth. Add a pinch or two of salt and pepper as you go, stirring occasionally until onions turn translucent.

Add the remaining ingredients --2 ½ boxes vegetable broth, kale and/or spinach, diced tomatoes, cannellini beans, corn, farro, and all seasonings.

Simmer on low for 30 minutes.

Nutrition Facts

Amount Per Serving

Calories 277

Total Fat 2.7g4%

Sodium 439mg18%

Total Carbohydrates 53g18%

Dietary Fiber 11.1g44%

Sugars 9.6g

Protein 12.4g25%

Calcium12%

Iron24%

Tomato, Carrot, Brussels Sprouts Soup

This heart-healthy, nutrient-rich soup recipe is not only chock-full of goodness but is so good tasting, too. Carrot juice adds a touch of sweetness and the Brussels sprouts are a unique addition.

Prep Time 25 minutes

Cook Time 30 minutes

Servings: 6 people

INGREDIENTS

1/4 cup low sodium vegetable broth (Trader Joe's brand) or water for sauteing (or 1/4 cup homemade)

1 medium onion chopped

5 cloves garlic minced

2 carrots peeled and cut into rounds

1 large beet peeled and cut into 1/2″ cubes

3 cups brussels sprouts cut in half or fourths

4 cups water or vegetable broth

2 cups carrot juice or vegetable broth

1/3 cup uncooked green lentils

1/2 cup uncooked red lentils

1/2 cup kidney beans no salt Eden brand

1 8 oz. can tomato sauce

1/3 tsp Ceylon cinnamon

1/2 tsp garam masala

2 Tbl almond or peanut butter

sea salt and pepper to taste

INSTRUCTIONS

In a large pot, sauté the onions and garlic in 1/4 cup of water or vegetable broth until wilted.

Add the cinnamon and garam masala and stir.

Add the rest of the chopped vegetables and sauté a few more minutes.

Add the red and green lentils, water or vegetable broth, carrot juice, tomato sauce, beans, and nut butter.

Simmer soup, covered for 30-45 minutes until the vegetables are crisp tender and the lentils are soft.

Season with salt and pepper to taste.

Nutrition Facts

Amount Per Serving

Calories 244Calories from Fat 35

Total Fat 3.9g6%

Total Carbohydrates 42.5g14%

112

Dietary Fiber 9.3g37%

Sugars 11.2g

Protein 12.7g25%

Calcium11%

Iron24%

Vegan Corn Chowder

So creamy and comforting, this vegan corn chowder is a crowd pleaser and taste flavor you're gonna love!

Prep Time 20 minutes

Cook Time 30 minutes

Servings 8 people

INGREDIENTS

1/4 cup water or vegetable broth, Trader Joe's Low Sodium

1 cup onion chopped finely

1 cup red bell pepper seeded and chopped (reserving 1/4 cup for garnish)

2 ribs celery chopped

2 cloves garlic minced

½ tsp red pepper flakes optional

1 medium potato peeled and diced

2 cups corn from 3 ears or frozen

2 Tbl nutritional yeast (optional)

½ tsp sea salt

2 cups low sodium vegetable broth (or 2 cups homemade)

1 cup unsweetened non-dairy milk

1 Tbl Capital Hill Seasoning (shallots, dill weed, parsley and chives) Not required, but tasty.

juice of ½ lemon

sea salt and pepper to taste

Garnish

fresh cilantro

green onion chopped

red pepper chopped

Vegan Corn Chowder

INSTRUCTIONS

In a large pot over medium heat, add ¼ cup water or vegetable broth and sauté onion, garlic, red pepper and celery for 10 minutes or until soft.
Add diced potato, vegetable broth, and non-dairy milk and mix well.
Add spices, nutritional yeast, and lemon and stir to combine. Bring to a boil. Once at a boil, reduce to simmer, cover the pan with a lid and simmer gently for 15-20 minutes, or until potatoes are tender.

Once the potatoes are tender, add corn kernels and stir to combine. Let cook for a further 5-10 minutes or until corn is tender to your liking.

Transfer about a third of the soup to a blender, and blend until smooth. Or use an immersion blender to cream part of the soup in the pot.

Pour back into the pot and stir well. Add salt and pepper to taste.

Top each serving with chopped green onion, cilantro and extra bits of corn and red pepper.

NUTRITION/NOTES

Amount Per Serving

Calories 92

Total Fat 2.1g3%

Sodium 217mg9%

Total Carbohydrates 16.9g6%

Sugars 5.3g

Protein 3.4g7%

Calcium3%

Iron5%

Vegan Sauerkraut Soup

Kick up your health with this immunity-boosting vegan sauerkraut soup. Using ingredients you probably have on hand, add any store-bought sauerkraut you like. Ready in a matter of minutes and tasty, to boot.

Prep Time 20 minutes

Cook Time 25 minutes

Servings 8 people

2 1/2 cups

INGREDIENTS

1 rib celery finely diced

1 medium onion finely diced

2 medium carrots thinly sliced

3 medium potatoes peeled, chopped 1/2" cubes

1/4 cup quinoa uncooked and rinsed

2-3 cups sauerkraut drained and rinsed

8 cups low sodium vegetable broth (or 8 cups homemade)

2 cups water

1, cup of cooked white beans drained and rinsed. Sometimes called white kidney beans or cannellini.

1 bay leaf

sea salt and pepper to taste

INSTRUCTIONS

In a large pot over medium heat, saute the finely chopped celery and onion in a small amount of vegetable broth or water until softened and golden, about 5 minutes.

Add sliced carrots, potatoes, quinoa, bay leaf, broth and water. Bring to a boil then reduce heat and simmer 15 minutes or until the vegetables are tender.

Add sauerkraut and white beans and continue to cook about 10 minutes.

Remove bay leaf and transfer about half of the soup, slightly cooled, into a blender and blend until smooth. Then pour back into the pot and stir well. Or use an immersion blender to cream part of the soup right in the pot.

Season soup with salt and pepper to taste.

Nutrition Facts

Amount Per Serving

Calories 180Calories from Fat 13

Total Fat 1.4g2%

Total Carbohydrates 36.7g12%

Dietary Fiber 9.7g39%

Sugars 6.8g

Protein 8g16%

Calcium13%

Iron18%

Total Time

Prep: 20 min. Cook: 6 hours

Makes

12 servings (3 quarts)

Ingredients

1 carton (32 ounces) chicken broth

1 can (28 ounces) diced tomatoes, undrained

1 can (15 to 15-1/2 ounces) cannellini beans, rinsed and drained

1 package (10 to 12 ounces) frozen cooked winter squash, thawed

1 package (10 ounces) frozen leaf spinach, thawed and squeezed dry

1-3/4 cups cubed fully cooked ham

3 medium carrots, peeled, chopped

1 large onion, chopped

3 garlic cloves, minced

1 teaspoon reduced-sodium seafood seasoning

1/4 teaspoon pepper

Grated Parmesan cheese, optional

Directions

In a 5- or 6-qt. slow cooker, combine all ingredients. Cook, covered, on low for 6-8 hours. If desired, sprinkle with Parmesan cheese.

Test Kitchen tips

To make Pasta e Fagioli, add ditalini or elbow pasta to this soup. For a spicy twist, sprinkle with hot sauce.

Nutrition Facts

1 cup: 102 calories, 1g fat (0 saturated fat), 14mg cholesterol, 808mg sodium, 15g carbohydrate (4g sugars, 4g fiber), 8g protein.

Vichyssoise with Fennel

This vichyssoise is a healthier, plant-based take on the traditional and is made creamy with cashews and unsweetened non-dairy milk.

Prep Time 15 minutes

Cook Time 10 minutes

Serving Size 6 people

1 1/2 Cups or 1 Bowl

INGREDIENTS

1 lb Yukon gold potatoes, about 3 medium

2 medium sized fennel bulbs washed and the stalks trimmed 1" above the bulb

½ yellow onion chopped or 3 large leeks, washed and white part sliced

3 cloves garlic chopped

1 1/2 cups unsweetened non-dairy milk soy, almond or oat or cashew (not coconut) (or 1 1/2 cups homemade)

1 1/2 quarts low sodium vegetable broth (or 1 1/2 qts homemade)

½ cup raw cashews soaked in hot water (optional)

1 sprig thyme

1/4 cup white wine (optional)

INSTRUCTIONS

If your pressure cooker has a saute function, turn it on, add the onion and fennel and begin to saute while you chop the potatoes.

Add the rest of the ingredients to the pot of the pressure cooker, except the non-dairy milk.

Use the manual setting and set for 10 minutes. After warming up, the timer will begin. When it's finished, either let cool manually or carefully release the pressure valve.

Using an immersion blender, blend the soup until smoothe (or use a blender) and add the non-dairy milk, stirring to combine. Top with chopped green onion or a little of a fennel frond.

Nutrition Facts

Amount Per Serving

Calories 270

Total Fat 11.3g17%

Total Carbohydrates 36.7g12%

Dietary Fiber 7.3g29%

Sugars 8.5g

Protein 9.1g18%

Calcium10%

Iron20%

Soup with Spinach

Toss in all of the ingredients and before you know it, yummy Italian Soup is served. Add a dollop of soy yogurt to make it creamy.

Prep Time 20 minutes

Cook Time 4 hours

Servings 6 people

© Copyright 2021 by Victoria Torres

INGREDIENTS

2 cloves garlic minced

1 small yellow onion diced

3 cups low sodium vegetable broth or water, (or 3 cups homemade)

1 14.5 oz can Italian-style diced tomatoes (no salt)

1 14.5 oz can fire-roasted diced tomatoes (no salt)

1 can pinto beans (no salt) drained and rinsed (or 1 1/2 cups homemade)

2 large carrots sliced

2 ribs celery sliced

2 small red potatoes ½" cubed

1 large green bell pepper chopped

1 tsp Italian seasoning

2 tsp dried oregano

1/2 - 1 Tbl dried basil

3/4 cup whole wheat Orzo pasta, uncooked

2-3 cups fresh spinach packed

128

sea salt and pepper to taste

INSTRUCTIONS

Into a large slow cooker, add the onion and the chopped garlic along with both cans of tomatoes (undrained), the beans, sliced carrots, sliced celery, red potatoes, and bell pepper and the water or vegetable broth.

Add in the seasonings: Italian seasoning, oregano, and basil. I add in salt and pepper to taste. Depending on the saltiness of the broth, you might want to completely omit salt.

Put the slow cooker on low for 8 hours or high for 4 hours.

After 8 hours (or 4 if you're on high), add the orzo pasta and cook another 20 minutes or until the orzo is done.

Then, gently stir in the spinach.

Taste and adjust seasonings to your preference.

Enjoy with crusty whole grain bread.

Nutrition Facts

Amount Per Serving

Calories 206

Total Fat 1.2g2%

Total Carbohydrates 41.8g14%

Dietary Fiber 10.1g40%

Sugars 9.5g

Protein 7.9g16%

Calcium14%

Iron22%

Mulligatawny Soup

Indian-spiced mulligatawny soup smells heavenly while cooking in your kitchen. Apple adds a touch of sweetness using lite coconut milk keeps the calories low.

Prep Time 20 minutes

Cook Time 30 minutes

Servings: 6 people

INGREDIENTS

1/4 cup low sodium vegetable broth or water for sauteeing

1 cup uncooked red lentils rinsed and cleaned

131

1 large yellow onion chopped

1 large carrot peeled and diced

2 small or 1 large potato peeled and diced

3 cloves garlic minced

2 tsp fresh ginger peeled and minced

1 large firm apple peeled, cored and diced

2 diced tomatoes

1 Tbl curry powder

1/2 tsp ground coriander

1/2 tsp ground cinnamon

1/2 tsp ground turmeric

1/4 tsp ground cardamom

1/4 tsp freshly ground black pepper

4 cups low sodium vegetable broth (or 4 cups homemade)

2/3 cup light canned coconut milk (or use 2/3 cup non-dairy milk mixed with about 1 tsp coconut extract)

sea salt and pepper to taste

1/3 cup cilantro chopped, and/or scallions for garnish

INSTRUCTIONS

Add the onion and carrot to a large pot with ¼ cup water or vegetable broth over medium heat, then sauté for 4 to 5 minutes, or until the onions have softened.

Add the potatoes, garlic, ginger, apples, and diced tomatoes to the pot. Sauté for another 3 minutes, then add all of the spices and toss to coat.

Add the lentils and broth and let the contents come to a boil. Turn the heat down to medium-low and simmer uncovered for 30 minutes. Add more water or broth if it gets too thick.

Transfer about half of the soup, slightly cooled, into a blender and blend until smooth. Then pour back into the pot and stir well. Or use an immersion blender to cream part of the soup in the pot.

Stir in the coconut milk and cook a few more minutes.

Taste, and adjust salt and black pepper as needed.

Serve topped with scallions along with crusty bread or naan for dipping.

Nutrition Facts

Amount Per Serving

Calories 256

Total Fat 7.9g12%

Total Carbohydrates 37.9g13%

Dietary Fiber 7.8g31%

Sugars 6.3g

Protein 10g20%

Calcium7%

Iron22%

Cauliflower Wedges

Total Time
Prep/Total Time: 30 min.

Makes
8 servings

This meal is incredibly easy, yet is packed with flavor and looks like a dish from a five-star restaurant. The grill leaves the cauliflower cooked but crisp, and the red pepper flakes add bite.

Ingredients

1 large head cauliflower

1 teaspoon ground turmeric

1/2 teaspoon crushed red pepper flakes

2 tablespoons olive oil

Lemon juice, additional olive oil and pomegranate seeds, optional

Directions

Remove leaves and trim stem from cauliflower. Cut cauliflower into eight wedges. Mix turmeric and pepper flakes. Brush wedges with oil; sprinkle with turmeric mixture.

Grill, covered, over medium-high heat or broil 4 in. from heat until cauliflower is tender, 8-10 minutes on each side. If desired, drizzle with lemon juice and additional oil and serve with pomegranate seeds.

Nutrition Facts

1 wedge: 57 calories, 4g fat (1g saturated fat), 0 cholesterol, 32mg sodium, 5g carbohydrate (2g sugars, 2g fiber), 2g protein. Diabetic Exchanges: 1 vegetable, 1 fat.

Roasted Pumpkin and Brussels Sprouts

Total Time
Prep: 15 min. Bake: 35 min.

Makes
8 servings

Ingredients
1 medium pie pumpkin (about 3 pounds), peeled and cut into 3/4-inch cubes
1 pound fresh Brussels sprouts, trimmed and halved lengthwise
4 garlic cloves, thinly sliced

© Copyright 2021 by Victoria Torres

1/3 cup olive oil

2 tablespoons balsamic vinegar

1 teaspoon sea salt

1/2 teaspoon coarsely ground pepper

2 tablespoons minced fresh parsley

Directions

Preheat oven to 400°. In a large bowl, combine pumpkin, Brussels sprouts and garlic. In a small bowl, whisk oil, vinegar, salt and pepper; drizzle over vegetables and toss to coat.

Transfer to a greased 15x10x1-in. baking pan. Roast 35-40 minutes or until tender, stirring once. Sprinkle with parsley.

Nutrition Facts

3/4 cup: 152 calories, 9g fat (1g saturated fat), 0 cholesterol, 255mg sodium, 17g carbohydrate (4g sugars, 3g fiber), 4g protein. Diabetic Exchanges: 2 fat, 1 starch.

Black Bean-Tomato Chili

Total Time
Prep: 10 min. Cook: 35 min.

Makes
6 servings (2-1/4 quarts)

Ingredients
2 tablespoons olive oil
1 large onion, chopped

1 medium green pepper, chopped

3 garlic cloves, minced

1 teaspoon ground cinnamon

1 teaspoon ground cumin

1 teaspoon chili powder

1/4 teaspoon pepper

3 cans (14-1/2 ounces each) diced tomatoes, undrained

2 cans (15 ounces each) black beans, rinsed and drained

1 cup orange juice or juice from 3 medium oranges

Directions

In a Dutch oven, heat oil over medium-high heat. Add onion and green pepper; cook and stir 8-10 minutes or until tender. Add garlic and seasonings; cook 1 minute longer.

Stir in remaining ingredients; bring to a boil. Reduce heat; simmer, covered, 20-25 minutes to allow flavors to blend, stirring occasionally.

Nutrition Facts

1-1/2 cups: 232 calories, 5g fat (1g saturated fat), 0 cholesterol, 608mg sodium, 39g carbohydrate (13g sugars, 10g fiber), 9g protein. Diabetic Exchanges: 2 vegetable, 1-1/2 starch, 1 lean meat, 1 fat.

Total Time

Prep: 10 min. Bake: 30 min.

Makes

6 servings

Ingredients

2 pounds small red potatoes, cut into wedges

2 tablespoons olive oil

3/4 teaspoon garlic pepper blend

1/2 teaspoon Italian seasoning

1/4 teaspoon salt

1/4 cup balsamic vinegar

Directions

Preheat oven to 425°. Toss potatoes with oil and seasonings; spread in a 15x10x1-in. pan.

Roast 25 minutes, stirring halfway. Drizzle with vinegar; roast until potatoes are tender, 5-10 minutes.

Nutrition Facts

3/4 cup: 159 calories, 5g fat (1g saturated fat), 0 cholesterol, 143mg sodium, 27g carbohydrate (4g sugars, 3g fiber), 3g protein. Diabetic Exchanges: 2 starch, 1 fat.

Confetti Quinoa

Total Time

Prep/Total Time: 30 min.

Makes

4 servings

Ingredients

2 cups water

1 cup quinoa, rinsed

1/2 cup chopped fresh broccoli

1/2 cup coarsely chopped zucchini

1/4 cup shredded carrots

1/2 teaspoon salt

1 tablespoon lemon juice

1 tablespoon olive oil

Directions

In a large saucepan, bring water to a boil. Add next five ingredients. Reduce heat; simmer, covered, until liquid is absorbed, 12-15 minutes. Stir in lemon juice and oil; heat through. Remove from heat; fluff with a fork.

Nutrition Facts

2/3 cup: 196 calories, 6g fat (1g saturated fat), 0 cholesterol, 307mg sodium, 29g carbohydrate (1g sugars, 4g fiber), 7g protein. Diabetic Exchanges: 2 starch, 1/2 fat.

Test Kitchen tips

Serve with cornbread or a French baguette.

Nutrition Facts

1-1/3 cups: 210 calories, 1g fat (0 saturated fat), 0 cholesterol, 463mg sodium, 42g carbohydrate (5g sugars, 7g fiber), 11g protein. Diabetic Exchanges: 3 starch, 1 lean meat.

Maple-Walnut Sweet Potatoes

Total Time

Prep: 15 min. Cook: 5 hours

Makes

12 servings

Ingredients

4 pounds sweet potatoes (about 8 medium)

3/4 cup coarsely chopped walnuts, divided

1/2 cup packed light brown sugar

1/2 cup dried cherries, coarsely chopped

1/2 cup maple syrup

145

1/4 cup apple cider or juice

1/4 teaspoon salt

Directions

Peel and cut sweet potatoes lengthwise in half; cut crosswise into 1/2-in. slices. Place in a 5-qt. slow cooker. Add 1/2 cup walnuts, brown sugar, cherries, syrup, cider and salt; toss to combine.

Cook, covered, on low 5-6 hours or until potatoes are tender. Sprinkle with remaining walnuts.

Nutrition Facts

3/4 cup: 298 calories, 5g fat (0 saturated fat), 0 cholesterol, 70mg sodium, 62g carbohydrate (37g sugars, 5g fiber), 4g protein.

Total Time

Prep/Total Time: 25 min.

Makes

6 servings

Ingredients

2 tablespoons olive oil

2 medium onions, chopped

6 garlic cloves, sliced

1/2 cup white balsamic vinegar

2 bunches Swiss chard, coarsely chopped (about 16 cups)

1/2 cup walnut halves, toasted

1/4 teaspoon salt

1/4 teaspoon pepper

Directions

In a 6-qt. stockpot, heat oil over medium-high heat. Add onions; cook and stir until tender. Add garlic; cook 1 minute longer.

Add vinegar, stirring to loosen any browned bits from pot. Add remaining ingredients; cook 4-6 minutes or until chard is tender, stirring occasionally.

Editor's Note

To toast nuts, bake in a shallow pan in a 350° oven for 5-10 minutes or cook in a skillet over low heat until lightly browned, stirring occasionally.

Nutrition Facts

2/3 cup: 159 calories, 10g fat (1g saturated fat), 0 cholesterol, 381mg sodium, 16g carbohydrate (9g sugars, 3g fiber), 4g protein. Diabetic Exchanges: 2 fat, 1 starch.

Hearty Vegetable Split Pea Soup

Total Time

Prep: 10 min. Cook: 7 hours

Makes

8 servings (2 quarts)

Ingredients

1 package (16 ounces) dried green split peas, rinsed

1 large carrot, chopped

1 celery rib, chopped

1 small onion, chopped

1 bay leaf

1-1/2 teaspoons salt

1/2 teaspoon dried thyme

1/2 teaspoon pepper

6 cups water

Directions

In a 3- or 4-qt. slow cooker, combine all ingredients. Cook, covered, on low 7-9 hours or until peas are tender. Stir before serving. Discard bay leaf.

Freeze option: Freeze cooled soup in freezer containers. To use, partially thaw in refrigerator overnight. Heat through in a saucepan, stirring occasionally; add water if necessary.

Nutrition Facts

1 cup: 202 calories, 1g fat (0 saturated fat), 0 cholesterol, 462mg sodium, 36g carbohydrate (5g sugars, 15g fiber), 14g protein. Diabetic exchanges: 2 starch, 1 lean meat.

Curried Lentil Soup

Curry gives a different taste sensation to this chili-like soup. It's delicious with a dollop of sour cream.

Total Time
Prep: 15 min. Cook: 8 hours

Makes
10 servings (2-1/2 quarts)

Ingredients
4 cups water
1 can (28 ounces) crushed tomatoes

3 medium potatoes, peeled and diced

3 medium carrots, thinly sliced

1 cup dried lentils, rinsed

1 large onion, chopped

1 celery rib, chopped

4 teaspoons curry powder

1-1/4 teaspoons salt

2 bay leaves

2 garlic cloves, minced

Directions

In a 4- or 5-qt. slow cooker, combine all ingredients. Cover and cook on low for 8 hours or until vegetables and lentils are tender. Discard bay leaves.

Nutrition Facts

1 cup: 148 calories, 1g fat (0 saturated fat), 0 cholesterol, 462mg sodium, 31g carbohydrate (6g sugars, 5g fiber), 7g protein. Diabetic Exchanges: 1-1/2 starch, 1 vegetable.

Roasted Tater Rounds with Green Onions & Tarragon

Total Time

Prep: 25 min. Broil: 10 min.

Makes

8 servings

Ingredients

4 pounds potatoes (about 8 medium), sliced 1/4 inch thick

Cooking spray

2 teaspoons sea salt

1 teaspoon coarsely ground pepper

6 green onions, thinly sliced (about 3/4 cup)

3 tablespoons minced fresh parsley

2 tablespoons minced fresh tarragon

Olive oil, optional

Directions

Preheat broiler. Place potatoes in a large microwave-safe bowl; spritz with cooking spray and toss to coat. Microwave, covered, on high 10-12 minutes or until almost tender, stirring halfway through cooking.

Spread potatoes into greased 15x10x1-in. baking pans. Spritz with additional cooking spray; sprinkle with salt and pepper.

Broil 4-6 in. from heat 10-12 minutes or until golden brown, stirring halfway through cooking. In a small bowl, mix green onions, parsley and tarragon. Sprinkle over potatoes; toss to coat. If desired, drizzle with olive oil.

Nutrition Facts

3/4 cup: 185 calories, 1g fat (0 saturated fat), 0 cholesterol, 497mg sodium, 41g carbohydrate (2g sugars, 5g fiber), 5g protein.

Quinoa Tabbouleh

Total Time

Prep: 35 min. + chilling

Makes

8 servings

Ingredients

2 cups water

1 cup quinoa, rinsed

1 can (15 ounces) black beans, rinsed and drained

1 small cucumber, peeled and chopped

1 small sweet red pepper, chopped

1/3 cup minced fresh parsley

1/4 cup lemon juice

2 tablespoons olive oil

1/2 teaspoon salt

1/2 teaspoon pepper

Directions

In a large saucepan, bring water to a boil. Add quinoa. Reduce heat; cover and simmer until liquid is absorbed, 12-15 minutes. Remove from the heat; fluff with a fork. Transfer to a bowl; cool completely.

Add the beans, cucumber, red pepper and parsley. In a small bowl, whisk the remaining ingredients; drizzle over salad and toss to coat. Refrigerate until chilled.

Editor's Note

Look for quinoa in the cereal, rice or organic food aisle.

Nutrition Facts

3/4 cup: 159 calories, 5g fat (1g saturated fat), 0 cholesterol, 255mg sodium, 24g carbohydrate (1g sugars, 4g fiber), 6g protein. Diabetic Exchanges: 1-1/2 starch, 1 fat.

Total Time
Prep/Total Time: 30 min.

Makes

4 servings

Ingredients

2 tablespoons canola oil

1 medium onion, finely chopped

1 medium sweet red pepper, finely chopped

1 celery rib, finely chopped

2 teaspoons chili powder

1/4 teaspoon salt

1/4 teaspoon pepper

2 cups vegetable stock

1 cup frozen corn

1 cup quinoa, rinsed

1 can (15 ounces) black beans, rinsed and drained

1/3 cup plus 2 tablespoons minced fresh cilantro, divided

Directions

In a large skillet, heat oil over medium-high heat. Add onion, red pepper, celery and seasonings; cook and stir 5-7 minutes or until vegetables are tender.

Stir in stock and corn; bring to a boil. Stir in quinoa. Reduce heat; simmer, covered, 12-15 minutes or until liquid is absorbed.

Add beans and 1/3 cup cilantro; heat through, stirring occasionally. Sprinkle with remaining cilantro.

Test Kitchen Tips

Quinoa (pronounced KEEN-wah) is an ancient South American grain. It's often referred to as the "the perfect grain" because, unlike other grains, it offers a complete protein. This makes quinoa an excellent choice for vegetarian and vegan meals, which can otherwise tend to be low in protein

158

Chili powder is a seasoning blend made primarily from dried chili peppers. Other ingredients commonly include garlic, onion, salt, oregano, cumin, coriander, cloves, cinnamon and even cocoa powder.

Explore all the delicious ways to make quinoa power bowls.

Editor's Note

Look for quinoa in the cereal, rice or organic food aisle.

Nutrition Facts

1-1/4 cups: 375 calories, 10g fat (1g saturated fat), 0 cholesterol, 668mg sodium, 60g carbohydrate (5g sugars, 10g fiber), 13g protein.

Total Time

Prep: 25 min. Cook: 1 hour 20 min.

Makes

16 servings (4 quarts)

Ingredients

1 tablespoon olive oil

8 medium carrots, sliced

2 large onions, chopped

4 celery ribs, chopped

1 large green pepper, seeded and chopped

1 garlic clove, minced

2 cups chopped cabbage

2 cups frozen cut green beans (about 8 ounces)

2 cups frozen peas (about 8 ounces)

1 cup frozen corn (about 5 ounces)

1 can (15 ounces) garbanzo beans or chickpeas, rinsed and drained

1 bay leaf

1-1/2 teaspoons dried parsley flakes

1 teaspoon salt

1 teaspoon dried marjoram

1 teaspoon dried thyme

1/2 teaspoon dried basil

1/4 teaspoon pepper

4 cups water

1 can (28 ounces) diced tomatoes, undrained

2 cups V8 juice

Directions

In a stockpot, heat oil over medium-high heat; saute carrots, onions, celery and green pepper until crisp-tender. Add garlic; cook and stir 1 minute. Stir in remaining ingredients; bring to a boil.

Reduce heat; simmer, covered, until vegetables are tender, 1 to 1-1/2 hours. Remove bay leaf.

Test Kitchen Tips

Peel onion; cut in half vertically. Leave root end intact. Place onion half flat side down on cutting board. Make several slices parallel to board into the onion, leaving root uncut. Then slice perpendicularly to chop the onion.

To keep parsley fresh for up to a month, trim the stems and place the bunch in a tumbler with an inch of water. Be sure no leaves are in the water. Tie a produce bag around the tumbler to trap humidity; store in the refrigerator. Each time you use the parsley, change the water and turn the produce bag inside out so any moisture that has built up inside the bag can escape.

Check out 40 veggie soup recipes that are sure to satisfy.

Nutrition Facts

1 cup: 105 calories, 2g fat (0 saturated fat), 0 cholesterol, 488mg sodium, 20g carbohydrate (9g sugars, 5g fiber), 4g protein. Diabetic Exchanges: 1 starch.

Total Time

Prep/Total Time: 30 min.

Makes

6 servings

Ingredients

1 pound bulk pork sausage

1 tablespoon canola oil

3 medium zucchini, thinly sliced

1 medium onion, chopped

1 can (14-1/2 ounces) stewed tomatoes, cut up

1 package (8.8 ounces) ready-to-serve long grain rice

1 teaspoon prepared mustard

1/2 teaspoon garlic salt

1/4 teaspoon pepper

1 cup Kerrygold shredded sharp cheddar cheese

Directions

In a large skillet, cook sausage over medium heat 5-7 minutes or until no longer pink, breaking into crumbles. Drain and remove sausage from pan.

In same pan, heat oil over medium heat. Add zucchini and onion; cook and stir 5-7 minutes or until tender. Stir in sausage, tomatoes, rice, mustard, garlic salt and pepper. Bring to a boil.

Reduce heat; simmer, covered, 5 minutes to allow flavors to blend.

Remove from heat; sprinkle with cheese. Let stand, covered, 5 minutes or until cheese is melted.

Nutrition Facts

1-1/3 cups: 394 calories, 26g fat (9g saturated fat), 60mg cholesterol, 803mg sodium, 24g carbohydrate (6g sugars, 2g fiber), 16g protein.

Sweet Potato and Pesto Slow-Cooker Bread

Total Time

Prep: 45 min. + rising Cook: 3 hours + cooling

Makes

1 loaf (12 slices)

Ingredients

1 package (1/4 ounce) active dry yeast

2/3 cup warm half-and-half cream (110° to 115°)

1 large egg, room temperature

1 cup canned sweet potato puree or canned pumpkin

1 teaspoon sugar

1 teaspoon kosher salt

1/4 teaspoon ground nutmeg

3-1/2 to 4 cups bread flour

1 container (7 ounces) refrigerated prepared pesto

1/2 cup plus 2 tablespoons grated Parmesan cheese, divided

Directions

Dissolve yeast in warm cream. In a large bowl, combine egg, sweet potato puree, sugar, salt, nutmeg, yeast mixture and 2 cups flour; beat on medium speed until smooth. Stir in enough remaining flour to form a soft dough (dough will be sticky).

Turn onto a lightly floured surface; knead until smooth and elastic, 6-8 minutes. Place in a greased bowl, turning once to grease the top. Cover and let rise in a warm place until doubled, about 1 hour.

Punch down dough. Turn onto a lightly floured surface; roll into a 18x9-in. rectangle. Spread pesto to within 1 in. of edges; sprinkle with 1/2 cup Parmesan. Roll up jelly-roll style, starting with a long side; pinch seam and ends to seal.

Using a sharp knife, cut roll lengthwise in half; carefully turn each half cut side up. Loosely twist strips around each other, keeping cut surfaces facing up. Shape into a coil; place on parchment paper. Transfer to a 6-qt. slow cooker; sprinkle with remaining 2 tablespoons Parmesan. Let rise until doubled, about 1 hour.

Cook, covered, on low until bread is lightly browned, 3 to 3-1/2. Remove from slow cooker and cool slightly before slicing.

Nutrition Facts

1 slice: 271 calories, 10g fat (3g saturated fat), 26mg cholesterol, 464mg sodium, 36g carbohydrate (3g sugars, 2g fiber), 8g protein.

Pressure Cooker Curried Pumpkin Risotto

Total Time

Prep: 10 min. Cook: 15 min.

Makes

6 servings

Ingredients

1 tablespoon olive oil

1 small onion, chopped

1 cup uncooked arborio rice

2 garlic cloves, minced

2 cups chicken stock

1/2 cup canned pumpkin

1 tablespoon curry powder

1-1/2 teaspoons minced fresh rosemary or 3/4 teaspoon dried rosemary, crushed

1/2 teaspoon salt

1/4 teaspoon pepper

Directions

Select saute setting on a 6-qt. electric pressure cooker. Adjust for medium heat; add oil. When oil is hot, cook and stir onion until crisp-tender, 5-7 minutes. Add rice and garlic; cook and stir until rice is coated, 1-2 minutes. Add stock; cook 1 minute, stirring to loosen browned bits from pan. Press cancel.

Stir in pumpkin, curry powder, rosemary, salt and pepper. Lock lid; close pressure-release valve. Adjust to pressure-cook on high for 7 minutes. Quick-release pressure. If desired, serve with additional minced rosemary.

Slow-cooker option: Heat oil in a 6-qt. slow cooker on high until hot. Add rice; stir to coat. Stir in remaining ingredients. Cook, covered, on low until rice is tender, 3-4 hours, stirring halfway.

Nutrition Facts

1/2 cup: 163 calories, 3g fat (0 saturated fat), 0 cholesterol, 369mg sodium, 30g carbohydrate (2g sugars, 2g fiber), 4g protein. Diabetic exchanges: 2 starch, 1/2 fat.

Carrot Spice Thumbprint Cookies

Total Time
Prep: 30 min. Bake: 10 min./batch + cooling

Makes
5 dozen

Ingredients
1 cup margarine, softened

1 cup sugar

1/2 cup packed brown sugar

2 large eggs, room temperature

171

2 teaspoons vanilla extract

3 cups all-purpose flour

1-1/2 teaspoons ground cinnamon

1 teaspoon baking powder

3/4 teaspoon salt

1/2 teaspoon baking soda

1/8 teaspoon ground cloves

1-1/2 cups shredded carrots

2/3 cup chopped walnuts, toasted

1/2 cup dried cranberries

FROSTING:

1/2 cup butter, softened

4 ounces cream cheese, softened

2 cups confectioners' sugar

1 teaspoon vanilla extract

Additional confectioners' sugar

Directions

Preheat oven to 375°. In a large bowl, cream margarine and sugars until light and fluffy. Beat in eggs and vanilla. In another bowl, whisk flour, cinnamon, baking powder, salt, baking soda and cloves; gradually beat into creamed mixture. Stir in carrots, walnuts and cranberries.

Drop dough by rounded tablespoonfuls 2 in. apart onto parchment-lined baking sheets. Press a deep indentation in center of each with the back of a 1/2-teaspoon measure.

Bake until edges begin brown, 10-12 minutes. Reshape indentations as needed. Cool on pans 5 minutes. Remove to wire racks to cool completely.

For frosting, beat butter, cream cheese, confectioners' sugar and vanilla until blended. To serve, fill each cookie with about 1-1/2 teaspoons frosting; sprinkle with additional confectioners' sugar. Refrigerate leftover filled cookies.

Nutrition Facts

1 cookie: 167 calories, 9g fat (3g saturated fat), 17mg cholesterol, 146mg sodium, 21g carbohydrate (14g sugars, 1g fiber), 2g protein.

Smoky Sweet Potato and Black Bean Enchiladas

Total Time

Prep Time: 25 min. Cook Time: 35 min.

Makes

6 servings

Ingredients

1 large sweet potato, cubed

1 small onion, chopped

1 small sweet red pepper, chopped

© Copyright 2021 by Victoria Torres

1/2 cup minced fresh cilantro

1 teaspoon smoked paprika

1/2 teaspoon garlic powder

1/2 teaspoon ground cumin

1/2 teaspoon ground coriander

1/2 teaspoon pepper

1 can (15 ounces) black beans, rinsed and drained

1 can (15 ounces) enchilada sauce

12 corn tortillas (6 inches), warmed

2 cups shredded Monterey Jack cheese, divided

Optional toppings: cubed avocado, sour cream, salsa, minced cilantro and hot sauce

Directions

Preheat oven to 375°. In a large saucepan, place steamer basket over 1 in. of water. Place sweet potato, onion and red pepper in basket. Bring water to a boil. Reduce heat to maintain a simmer; steam, covered, until tender, about 15-20 minutes.

Transfer vegetables to a large bowl. Mash vegetables, gradually adding cilantro, spices and pepper to reach desired consistency. Stir in black beans.

Spread 1/3 cup enchilada sauce into a greased 13x9-in. baking dish. Place 1/3 cup vegetable mixture in center on each tortilla; sprinkle with 4 teaspoons cheese. Roll up and place in prepared dish, seam side down. Top with remaining enchilada sauce; sprinkle with remaining cheese.

Bake, uncovered, 20-25 minutes or until heated through and cheese is melted. If desired, serve with optional toppings.

Freeze option: Cover and freeze unbaked enchiladas. To use, partially thaw in refrigerator overnight. Remove from refrigerator 30 minutes before baking. Preheat oven to 375°. Cover casserole with foil; bake until casserole is heated through, sauce is bubbling and cheese is melted, 30-35 minutes. Serve as directed.

Test Kitchen tips

Short on time? This recipe can be made ahead of time. Just refrigerate the assembled (and unbaked) enchiladas for up to a week, and bake when ready. You can also freeze them for up to six months, then defrost and bake when ready.

Like things spicy? Add 1/4 teaspoon cayenne pepper to the sweet potato mixture, and use a spicy enchilada sauce.

Nutrition Facts

2 enchiladas: 399 calories, 14g fat (7g saturated fat), 34mg cholesterol, 843mg sodium, 52g carbohydrate (9g sugars, 8g fiber), 18g protein.

Beets in Orange Sauce

Total Time

Prep: 15 min. Cook: 35 min.

Makes

8 servings

Ingredients

8 whole fresh beets

1/4 cup sugar

2 teaspoons cornstarch

Dash pepper

1 cup orange juice

1 medium navel orange, halved and sliced, optional

1/2 teaspoon grated orange zest

Directions

Place beets in a large saucepan; cover with water. Bring to a boil. Reduce heat; cover and cook for 25-30 minutes or until tender. Drain and cool slightly. Peel and slice; place in a serving bowl and keep warm.

In a small saucepan, combine the sugar, cornstarch and pepper; stir in orange juice until smooth. Bring to a boil; cook and stir for 2 minutes or until thickened. Remove from the heat; stir in orange slices if desired and zest. Pour over beets.

Editor's Note: A 15-ounce can of sliced beets may be substituted for the fresh beets. Drain the canned beets and omit the first step of the recipe.

Nutrition Facts

1 cup: 63 calories, 0 fat (0 saturated fat), 0 cholesterol, 39mg sodium, 15g carbohydrate (12g sugars, 1g fiber), 1g protein.

COCONUT-CRUSTED CHICKEN FINGERS WITH HONEY DIJON DIP

Prep Time: 20 mins

Cook Time: 15 mins

Serves: 2

Ingredients

For the Chicken Fingers:

2 medium skinless chicken breasts (sliced lengthwise into ½" strips)

½ cup + 2 T coconut flour

¼ cup coconut flakes (unsweetened and shredded)

1 large egg (room temperature)

½ t paprika

½ t garlic powder

179

¼ t cayenne pepper

1 T avocado oil

Salt & pepper to taste

For the Dipping Sauce:

4 T Dijon mustard

1 T avocado oil

¼ cup coconut cream or Paleo mayo

2 T honey

½ t paprika

Instructions

Preheat oven to 375°F.

Prepare a baking sheet with parchment paper. Then sprinkle it with half of the shredded coconut flakes. Set aside.

In a small bowl, combine the ingredients for the dipping sauce. Then sprinkle the paprika on top of them. Set it in the refrigerator, so the flavors can marry.

In a small bowl, add the egg to 2-3 tablespoons water. Whisk for a few minutes. Set aside.

In a separate small bowl, combine the coconut flour with the salt, pepper, and other seasonings.

Dip each chicken breast into the egg wash. Then immediately dip it into the flour mixture, and generously coat it.

Place the shredded coconut flakes on the baking sheet. Then place each chicken piece on top of the flakes. Sprinkle the remaining coconut flakes on top of the chicken pieces. Note: chicken should be room temperature 20 minutes before baking.

Drizzle each piece with the avocado oil.

Bake for 15 minutes.

Immediately turn the broiler on high. Cook another 2-3 minutes, until brown and crispy.

Let cool 5 minutes, and serve with the honey Dijon dipping sauce.

SPICY PINEAPPLE CHICKEN TENDERS

Prep Time: 30 mins

Cook Time: 15 mins

Serves: 4

Ingredients

For the Chicken Tenders

1 lb chicken strips

½ cup coconut flour

2 t cayenne pepper

½ t salt

2 eggs

2 cups unsweetened shredded coconut

3 T coconut oil + more for drizzling over

Chopped fresh parsley, for garnishing

For the Pineapple Sauce

2 cups cubed pineapple (either fresh or canned is fine)

1 T coconut oil

1 T coconut aminos

1 T grated ginger

3 large garlic cloves, minced

½ cup water

Dash of cayenne powder, for sprinkling over the sauce

Instructions

Preheat the oven to 400 °F and lightly grease a baking sheet with coconut oil.

Rinse the chicken strips and use paper towels to dry them.

In a shallow dish, mix the coconut flour, cayenne powder, and salt to combine.

In another shallow dish, break the eggs and beat well. Pour the shredded coconut into a third shallow dish.

Lightly coat the chicken strips in the coconut flour mixture, making sure to shake off any excess flour. Then dip the chicken strips in the beaten eggs before coating them in the shredded coconut.

Place the coconut-coated chicken strips in a single layer on the prepared baking sheet, leaving at least 2 inches between each piece of chicken. Drizzle a bit of coconut oil over the chicken strips.

Bake for 15 minutes or until golden brown on both sides, flipping over halfway through.

While the chicken is baking, prepare the pineapple sauce. Combine the coconut oil, coconut aminos, cubed pineapple, grated ginger, minced garlic, and water in a large skillet.

Bring the ingredients to a boil before reducing to a simmer for a couple of minutes. Remove the skillet from heat, allow the ingredients to cool, and then process the ingredients in an electric blender until smooth.

Sprinkle a dash of cayenne powder over the pineapple sauce. Serve with the crispy coconut chicken tenders garnished with chopped fresh parsley.

Tips:

If you don't have coconut flour, you can easily substitute tapioca flour.

If you don't like spicy foods, leave out the cayenne powder and replace with garlic powder or onion powder.

SPICY AVOCADO EGG SALAD

Prep Time: 5 minutes

Servings: 1

Ingredients

1 hard-boiled egg

2 tsp guacamole

1 tsp mayonnaise

salt and pepper

Instructions

Prepare your hard boiled eggs the day before to save yourself some time.

I like to use an egg slicer to dice my egg – one set of cuts in the wide direction, then carefully re-positioned and cut again the long way.

The next part is easy – combine all the ingredients together and add salt and pepper to taste!

THE ULTIMATE MONTE CRISTO RECIPE

Prep Time: 5 minutes

Cook Time: 10 minutes

Servings: 2

Ingredients

6 pancakes from my cream cheese pancake recipe

4 slices of turkey

4 slices of ham

2 cups shredded swiss cheese

low carb, sugar-free maple syrup

Instructions

First, make six pancakes from my cream cheese pancake recipe. Once the pancakes are ready, separate the turkey and ham into four piles with two slices each. Two piles of turkey with two slices, and two piles of ham with two slices. Add 1/2 cup of swiss cheese to each pile. Cook on medium-low in the same pan that you cooked the pancakes, add a little more coconut oil and cover with a lid until the cheese is melted.

Prep Time: 3 minutes

Cook Time: 2 minutes

Servings: 1

Ingredients

marinara sauce

1 slice of provolone cheese

italian seasoning

a sprinkle of shaved parmesan cheese

Instructions

It all starts with my favorite low carb meatballs, which are pretty much carbless anyway, topped with a naturally low-carb sauce (there are so many these days!) then topped with some shaved parmesan and Italian seasoning, on a sub of provolone cheese.

188

When using cheese as the "wrap" on hot/warm sandwiches, you can use provolone because it's usually cut thick and can hold up under heat pretty well.

To pack this ahead of time, just get some of those Lunch Blox and separate your meatballs from your provolone. Then, just roll them up at work!

KETO INSTANT POT CRACK CHICKEN

Prep time: 5 mins

Cook time: 20 mins

Serves: 8 (yields about 7 cups total)

Ingredients

2 slices bacon, chopped

2 lbs (910 g) boneless, skinless chicken breasts

189

2 (8 oz/227 g) blocks cream cheese

½ cup (120 ml) water

2 tablespoons apple cider vinegar

1 tablespoon dried chives

1½ teaspoons garlic powder

1½ teaspoons onion powder

1 teaspoon crushed red pepper flakes

1 teaspoon dried dill

¼ teaspoon salt

¼ teaspoon black pepper

½ cup (2 oz/57 g) shredded cheddar

1 scallion, green and white parts, thinly sliced

Instructions

Turn pressure cooker on, press "Sauté", and wait 2 minutes for the pot to heat up. Add the chopped bacon and cook until crispy. Transfer to a plate and set aside. Press "Cancel" to stop sautéing. Add the chicken, cream cheese, water, vinegar, chives, garlic powder, onion powder, crushed red pepper flakes, dill, salt, and black pepper to the pot. Turn the pot on Manual, High Pressure for 15 minutes and then do a quick release.

Use tongs to transfer the chicken to a large plate, shred it with 2 forks, and return it back to the pot.

Stir in the cheddar cheese.

Top with the crispy bacon and scallion, and serve.

BACON CHEDDAR CHIVE OMELETTE

INGREDIENTS

• 2 slices Bacon, already cooked

• 1 tsp. Bacon Fat

- 2 large Eggs

- 1 oz. Cheddar Cheese

- 2 stalks Chives

- Salt and Pepper to Taste

INSTRUCTION

1. Make sure that you have all of your ingredients ready to go as the omelette will cook quickly. Shred the cheese, pre-cook the bacon, and have the chives chopped (or use herb scissors).

2. Heat a pan with bacon fat in it to medium-low heat. You want it emitting a decent amount of heat when you hover your hand above the pan. Add the eggs, and season with chives, salt, and pepper.

3. Once the edges are starting to set, add your bacon to the center and let cook for 20-30 seconds longer. Then, turn the heat off on the stove.

4. Add the cheese on top of the bacon, making sure it's centered. Then, take two edges of the omelette and fold them onto the cheese. Hold the edges there for a moment as the cheese has to partially melt to act as a "glue" to hold them in place.

5. Do the same with the other edges, creating a burrito of sorts, then flip over and let cook in the now warm pan for a little longer.

6. Serve with a bit of extra cheese, bacon, and chives on top if you'd like – but by itself it's just plain delicious.

This makes 1 serving of Bacon Cheddar Chive Omelette.

The macros come out to be 463 Calories, 39g Fats, 1g Net Carbs, and 24g Protein.

INGREDIENTS

The Pancake Bun

• 0.75 oz. Pork Rinds

• 1 tbsp. Almond Flour

• 1 large Egg, beaten

• 1 tbsp. Heavy Cream

• 1/4 tsp. Vanilla Extract

• 2 tbsp. Maple Syrup

The Filling

- 2 oz. Hot Sausage

- 1 slice Cheddar Cheese

- 1 large Egg

INSTRUCTION

1. Measure out 2 Oz. Sausage and set aside. You can use a silicone ring mold from Amazon to help with the whole process to keep everything the same size.

2. Grind pork rinds in a food processor until a powder is formed.

3. Heat a pan to medium high heat on the stove. Add sausage in ring mold and cook until medium-well temperature. Once cooked, set aside in some foil to rest.

4. While the sausage is cooking, mix together pork rinds with all bun ingre-dients.

5. Put an egg ring mold inside the pan and fill 3/4 of the way with bun batter (this should be half of the batter).

6. Once the bun is browned on the bottom, remove the ring mold and flip to the other side. Cook until this side is also browned. Repeat the process with the other half of the batter to create another bun.

7. In the same pan, add an egg to the ring mold and lightly scramble. Cook completely until solidified.

8. Assemble together with 1 bun on bottom, 1 slice of cheese, hot egg, sausa-ge, and the last bun on top. Then, serve!

This yeilds 1 serving of Low Carb Pancake Sandwich.

It comes out to be 657 Calories, 55.7g Fats, 2.7g Net Carbs, and 40g Protein.

BACON AVOCADO MUFFINS

INGREDIENTS

- 5 Large Eggs

- 5 Slices Bacon

- 2 tbsp. Butter

- 1/2 cup Almond Flour

- 1/4 cup Flaxseed Meal

- 1 1/2 tbsp. Psyllium Husk

Powder

- 2 medium Avocados

- 4.5 oz. Colby Jack Cheese

- 3 medium Spring Onions

- 1 tsp. Minced Garlic

- 1 tsp. Dried Cilantro

- 1 tsp. Dried Chives

- 1/4 tsp. Red Chili Flakes

- Salt and Pepper to Taste

- 1 1/2 cup Coconut Milk (from the carton)

- 1 1/2 tbsp. Lemon Juice

- 1 tsp. Baking Powder

INSTRUCTION

1. In a bowl, mix together eggs, almond flour, flax, psyllium, spices, coconut

milk and lemon juice. Leave to sit while you cook the bacon.

2. In a pan over medium-low heat, cook the bacon until crisp. Add the butter to the pan when it's almost done cooking.

3. Chop the spring onions and grate the cheese. Add the spring onions,

cheese, and baking powder. Then, crumble the bacon and add all of the fat

to the mixture.

4. Slice an avocado in half, remove the pit, and then cube the avocado while

it's in the shell. Be careful of the sharp knife as you do this. Scoop out the

avocado and fold into the mixture gently.

5. Preheat oven to 350F, measure out batter into a cupcake tray that's been

sprayed or greased and bake for 24-26 minutes. You should have leftover batter to make 4 more muffins, which you can do at the same time or afterward.

6. Store on the fridge and enjoy cold!

This makes a total of 16 Avocado Bacon Muffins.

Each muffin comes out to be 163 Calories, 14.1g Fats, 1.5g Net Carbs, and 6.1g Protein.

INGREDIENTS

The Waffles

• 1/2 cup Almond Flour

• 2 tbsp. Flaxseed Meal

• 1/3 cup Coconut Milk

• 1 tsp. Vanilla Extract

• 1 tsp. Baking Powder

• 2 large Eggs

• 2 tbsp. Swerve

• 7 drops Liquid Stevia

The Filling

- 1/2 cup Raspberries

- Zest of 1/2 Lemon

- 1 tbsp. Lemon Juice

- 2 tbsp. Butter

- 1 tbsp. Swerve

- 3 oz. Double Cream Brie

INSTRUCTION

1. Mix together all of the ingredients for the waffles in a container. Make sure that the consistency is smooth and there are no lumps.

2. Heat a waffle maker and once hot, add your batter.

Allow it to cook until the light turns green or the steam levels are low.

3. Take the waffles out and allow them to cool slightly.

4. Slice your brie and lay on top of the waffles while still warm so that the brie comes to room temperature.

5. In a pan on the stove, heat butter and swerve. You can powder the swerve

in a spice grinder.

6. Once the butter is starting to brown and the swerve is dissolving, add your raspberries, lemon juice, and zest of 1/2 lemon.

7. Continue to stir the mixture until it bubbles and becomes jam-like.

8. Under the broiler, broil the brie until melted and the waffle slightly crisp.

9. Assemble the waffle together with the raspberry filling and the brie. Put into a pan and "grill" for 1-2 minutes per side.

10. Enjoy this delicious treat, or share!

This makes 2 servings of Raspberry Brie Grilled Waffles.

Each serving comes out to be 489 Calories, 39.5g Fats, 7g Net Carbs, and 21g Protein.

CINNAMON ROLL "OATMEAL"

INGREDIENTS

• 1 cup Crushed Pecans

• 1/3 cup Flax Seed Meal

• 1/3 cup Chia Seeds

• 1/2 cup Cauliflower, riced (~ 3 oz.)

• 3 1/2 cups Coconut Milk

• 1/4 cup Heavy Cream

• 3 oz. Cream Cheese

• 3 tbsp. Butter

- 1 1/2 tsp. Cinnamon

- 1 tsp. Maple Flavor

- 1/2 tsp. Vanilla

- 1/4 tsp. Nutmeg

- 1/4 tsp. Allspice

- 3 tbsp. Erythritol, powdered

- 10-15 drops Liquid Stevia

- 1/8 tsp. Xanthan Gum (optional)

INSTRUCTION

1. Measure out chia seeds and 1/3 cup flax seeds (ground) and set aside.

2. Rice 1/2 cup of cauliflower in a food processor. Set aside for a moment.

3. Add 1 cup raw pecans to a ziploc bag and use a rolling pin to crush them.

4. Make sure they're not too small, because you want them to add texture to

the dish.

5. Add pecans to a pan over low heat to toast.

6. In a saucepan, heat 3 1/2 cups coconut milk. Once warm, add cauliflower

and continue to cook until it starts to boil.

7. Turn the heat down to medium-low and add your seasonings: 1 1/2 tsp.

cinnamon, 1 tsp. maple flavor, 1/2 tsp. vanilla, 1/4 tsp. Nutmeg, and 1/4 tsp.

Allspice.

8. In a spice grinder, grind 3 tbsp. erythritol until it is completely powdered.

9. Add erythritol and 10-15 drops liquid stevia to the pan and stir in well.

10. Add the flaxseed meal and chia seed to the pan and mix well. This will start to thicken tremendously.

11. Measure out 1/4 cup heavy cream, 3 tbsp. butter, and 3 oz. Cream Cheese.

12. Once your mixture is hot again, add the toasted pecans, cream, butter, and cream cheese. Mix together well. Here, you can add 1/8 tsp. xanthan gum if you would like it to be a bit thicker. Enjoy!

This makes 6 total servings of Cinnamon Roll "Oatmeal".

Each serving comes out to be 398 Calories, 37.7g Fats, 3.1g Net Carbs, and 8.8g Protein.

INGREDIENTS

• 4 slices Bacon

• 5 large Eggs

• 1.5 oz. Pork Rinds

• 1 medium Tomato

• 1 medium Avocado

• 2 medium Jalapeno Pe-ppers, de-seeded

• 1/4 medium Onion

• 1/4 cup Cilantro, chopped

• Salt and Pepper to Taste

INSTRUCTION

1. Dice all of your vegetables to prep for the rest of the recipe. That's 1 tomato, 2 jalapeno peppers (de-seeded), and 1/4 medium onion.

2. Start by frying the 4 slices of bacon in a pan. Once they're done, remove them and place on paper towels for later. Make sure you keep as much fat in the pan as possible.

3. "Fry" 1.5 oz. pork rinds in the bacon fat. Make sure all of the pork rinds are coated properly.

4. Once the pork rinds are as crispy as you want them, add the vegetables to the pan. Mix everything together and season as needed.

5. Once the onions are almost translucent, add 1/4 cup chopped cilantro to the pan. Mix everything together.

6. Add 5 large eggs to the pan, pre-scrambled, and mix everything together.

7. Season as needed.

208

8. Let this cook like an omelette, and when ready, mix once to let the un-cooked egg go to the bottom of the pan.

9. Cube an avocado just before serving and fold into the mixture.

10. Serve up some delicious food!

This makes 3 total servings of Chicharrones con Huevos.

Each serving comes out to be 508 Calories, 43g Fats, 5g Net Carbs, and 24.7g Protein.

MAPLE PECAN FAT BOMB BARS

INGREDIENTS

- 2 cups Pecan Halves

- 1 cup Almond Flour

- 1/2 cup Golden Flaxseed Meal

- 1/2 cup Unsweetened Shredded Coconut

- 1/2 cup Coconut Oil

- 1/4 cup "Maple Syrup"

- 1/4 tsp. Liquid Stevia (~25 drops)

INSTRUCTION

1. Measure out 2 cups of pecan halves and bake for 6-8 minutes at 350F in the oven. Just enough to when they start becoming aromatic.

2. Remove pecans from the oven, then add to a plastic bag. Use a rolling pin to crush them into chunks. It doesn't matter too much about the consistency, but I like to get relatively large chunks so I can see them in the bars as I eat it.

3. Mix the dry ingredients into a bowl: 1 cup Almond Flour, 1/2 cup Golden Flaxseed Meal, and 1/2 cup Unsweetened Shredded Coconut.

4. Add the crushed pecans to the bowl and mix together again.

5. Finally, add the 1/2 cup Coconut Oil, 1/4 cup "Maple Syrup", and 1/4 tsp. Liquid Stevia. Mix this together well until a crumbly dough is for-med.

6. Press the dough into a casserole dish.

7. Bake for 20-25 minutes at 350F, or until the edges are lightly browned.

8. Remove from the oven, allow to partially cool, and refrigerate for at least 1 hour (to cut cleanly).

9. Cut into 12 slices and remove using a spatula.

This makes 12 total servings of Maple Pecan Fat Bomb Bars.

Each serving comes out to be 303 Calories, 30.5g Fats, 2g Net Carbs, and 4.9g Protein.

INGREDIENTS

• 3 tbsp. Olive Oil

• 1/2 medium Onion, diced

• 1 1/2 tsp. Garlic, minced

• 6 oz. Ham Steak, cooked and cubed

• 1 tbsp. Butter, to grease ramekins

• 6 large Eggs

• 1 cup Cheddar Cheese, shredded

- 1/2 cup Heavy Cream

- 2-3 tbsp. Fresh Chives, chopped

- 1/2 tsp. Kosher Salt

- 1/4 tsp. Black Pepper

INSTRUCTION

1. Preheat your oven to 400F. Prep all of your ingredients. Cube 6 oz. Cooked Ham Steak, dice 1/2 medium onion, mince 1 1/2 tsp. garlic, shred 1 cup of cheddar cheese, and chop 2-3 tbsp. fresh chives.

2. In a pan, heat olive oil. Once hot, add onions and let saute until soft.

3. Once soft, add garlic and continue sauteing until garlic is lightly browned.

4. In a bowl, add 6 eggs, 1/2 cup heavy cream, chopped chives, 1/2 tsp. salt, 1/4 tsp. pepper.

5. Add all of the other ingredients, including onion and garlic from the pan.

6. Mix together well.

7. Bake in the oven for 20 minutes or until puffed and lightly browned on the top.

8. Let cool slightly and serve!

This makes a total of 5 servings.

Each serving comes out to 404 Calories, 39.6g Fats, 3.5g Net Carbs, and 19.6g Protein.

Warm and cozy and oh so satisfying this easy-to-make lentil soup has potatoes and kale to up your nutrient quotient.

Prep Time 30 minutes

Cook Time 30 minutes

Serving Size 6 people

About 1 1/2 Cups

INGREDIENTS

2 cups cooked "regular" brown lentils or 1 cup uncooked

½ large onion chopped

3 cloves garlic peeled and minced

3 medium carrots peeled and chopped

2 stalks celery chopped

4 cups low sodium vegetable broth (or 4 cups homemade)

2 cups water

½ 6 oz. can tomato paste

½ tsp coriander

½ tsp cumin

½ tsp sea salt or to taste

¼ tsp freshly ground pepper

1 large potato peeled and chopped

2-3 large leaves kale stems removed and roughly chopped

INSTRUCTIONS

Add ¼ cup of water or veggie broth to a large pot and saute the onion, carrot, celery and garlic for several minutes until they start to wilt.

Add a little more broth along with the tomato paste and mix in the paste.

Add the remainder of the ingredients, except the kale, and stir to combine.

If you are using uncooked lentils, rinse and pick over and add them to the pot along with 2 extra cups of broth or water.

Cook on medium for about 20 minutes.

Add the kale, stir, and continue to cook for another 10-20 minutes or until the kale and lentils are soft.

NUTRITION/NOTES

Amount Per Serving (1 1/2 Cupsg)

Calories 187

Total Fat 0.7g1%

Total Carbohydrates 36.4g12%

Dietary Fiber 7.2g29%

Sugars 6.9g

Protein 10.9g22%

Calcium9%

Iron19%

Cauliflower Chowder

This cauliflower chowder also uses otherveggies like carrot, onions, and chickpeas, potatoes and soaked cashews to bring its delicious creamy consistency without using any dairy.

Prep Time 30 minutes

Cook Time 10 minutes

Servings 4 people

1 bowl

INGREDIENTS

1/2 cup raw cashews soaked in hot water for at least an hour

1 head cauliflower

1 medium onion chopped

1 regular size potato peeled and cut into cubes

2 large carrots peeled and chopped

1 bulb garlic

1/2 cup chickpeas no salt added (Eden Brand)

4 cups low sodium vegetable broth Trader Joe's brand, (or 4 cups homemade)

1/4-1/2 cup nutritional yeast

1 tsp sea salt or to taste

1/2 tsp ground pepper

1 large lemon juiced

1/3 tsp cayenne pepper or Tabasco

INSTRUCTIONS

Add cashews to a bowl, cover with hot water and let soak for at least 1 hour.

While cashews are soaking, preheat the oven to 425°F. Chop cauliflower into florets. Arrange on a baking sheet along with the carrots, potatoes, and season with salt and pepper.

Cut the top off the garlic bulb so that some of the cloves are slightly exposed. Season with salt and pepper. Wrap bulb in tin foil and place on sheet with vegetables.

Roast for 20−25 minutes until the cauliflower is starting to brown and the vegetables are soft. Allow the veggies to cool then add them to a high powered blender. Squeeze the garlic out of it's skin and add it to the blender, as well.

Drain and rinse the cashews, adding them to the blender along with the chick peas and nutritional yeast.

Pour in vegetable stock, lemon juice, cayenne pepper and additional salt and pepper, and blend on high until smooth and creamy. Taste and adjust seasonings as desired.

Pour into a large pot and simmer to heat through, adding more water as necessary to thin.

NUTRITION/NOTES

Salt not included

Nutrition Facts

Amount Per Serving

Calories 345

Total Fat 13.8g21%

Total Carbohydrates 44.9g15%

Dietary Fiber 11g44%

Sugars 12g

Protein 16g32%

Calcium12%

Iron25%

Easy Chana Masala With Chickpeas & Yams

This easy 1-pot chana masala is super flavorful and one of the most popular dishes in India. A healthy, plant-based, vegan meal.

Prep Time 10 minutes

Cook Time 30 minutes

Serving Size: 4 people

about 2 cups

INGREDIENTS

1 red onion diced

1 15 oz can chickpeas rinsed and drained

5 cloves garlic minced

2 tsp ginger minced

3 Tbl tomato paste

1 Tbl curry

1 tsp ground cumin

1 tsp coriander

2 tsp garam masala

1/8 tsp cayenne pepper

1 tsp paprika

1 tsp sea salt , optional

3/4 cup light canned coconut milk Trader Joe's brand

OR 1/2 tsp coconut extract mixed with 3/4 cup non-dairy milk, MALK brand

2 small yams or potatoes chopped

1 1/2 cup frozen peas

1 28 oz can diced tomatoes

INSTRUCTIONS

Saute onions, garlic and ginger in a small amount of water or stock on medium-low heat about 5 minutes until they start to soften and the liquid is almost evaporated.

Add the spices and cook with the onion mixture for another minute.

Add the tomato paste and coconut milk. Stir to combine.

Add chickpeas, potatoes and frozen peas and the whole can of diced tomatoes including the juice.

Cover and simmer until the potatoes are tender, about 25 minutes.

Serve topped with yogurt, bananas, chopped almonds or raisins and mango chutney.

NUTRITION/NOTES

does not include salt

Nutrition Facts

Amount Per Serving

Calories 311Calories from Fat 39

Total Fat 4.3g7%

Saturated Fat 2.4g12%

Cholesterol 0mg0%

Sodium 175mg7%

Total Carbohydrates 52g17%

Dietary Fiber 12g48%

Sugars 18g

Protein 12g24%

Vitamin A51%

Vitamin C32%

Calcium10%

Iron23%

Moroccan Stew with Kale

This hearty vegan stew is packed full chickpeas, lentils and kale with a touch of sweetness from dried apricots. Nutrient-dense and full of flavor!

Prep Time 30 minutes

Cook Time 30 minutes

Servings 6 People

1 bowl

INGREDIENTS

1/4 cup low sodium vegetable broth or water for sauteing

2 tsp ground cinnamon

2 tsp ground cumin

1 tsp ground ginger

1/2 tsp ground cloves

1/2 tsp ground nutmeg

1/2 tsp ground turmeric

1/2 tsp curry powder

1 tsp sea salt optional

1 large sweet onion chopped

2 cups rough chopped kale

4 cups (1, 32oz box) low sodium vegetable broth or more, (or 4 cups homemade)

1 14.5 oz can diced tomatoes undrained

4 large carrots chopped

2 medium sweet potatoes peeled and chopped

3 large potatoes peeled and chopped I used yukon golds

1 15 oz can garbanzo beans drained

1/2 cup dried apricots chopped

1 cup dried lentils rinsed

sea salt and pepper to taste

INSTRUCTIONS

Cook onion in a large pot on medium high heat in ¼ cup of water or vegetable broth until soft and just beginning to brown, 5 to 10 minutes. Stir in the spices and cook until they are fragrant.

Pour the vegetable broth into the pot. Add more if you want it to be more soup-like.

Stir in the tomatoes, carrots, sweet potatoes, potatoes, garbanzo beans, apricots, and lentils. Bring to a boil and reduce heat to low.

Stir in the shredded kale and simmer stew for 30 minutes until the vegetables and lentils are cooked and tender.

Season with salt and black pepper.

Simmer until stew has thickened, about 5 minutes.

NUTRITION/NOTES

salt not included in

Amount Per Serving

Calories 436

Total Fat 1.5g2%

Total Carbohydrates 91.6g31%

Dietary Fiber 14.2g57%

Sugars 18g

Protein 17.7g35%

Calcium16%

Iron34%

Irish Cabbage Potato Soup with Dumplings

This Irish Cabbage Soup is filled with potatoes, carrots and cabbage and a simple vegetable stock. After making in the Instant Pot, you will cook the whole wheat dumplings and serve straight from the pot.

Prep Time 25 minutes

Cook Time 30 minutes

Servings 6

INGREDIENTS

1/4 cup low sodium vegetable broth or water

1 medium onion chopped

3 cloves garlic crushed

1/2 green cabbage sliced

2 medium potatoes peeled and chopped

4 carrots peeled and chopped

1 bay leaf

1/2 tsp fresh thyme

2 Tbl nutritional yeast optional

6 cups low sodium vegetable broth (or 6 cups homemade)

sea salt and pepper to taste

Dumplings

1 cup whole wheat flour

2 tsp baking powder

1/2 tsp sea salt (optional)

1 Tbl fresh parsley chopped finely or ½ Tablespoon dried rosemary

1/2 cup all-purpose flour

3/4 cup non-dairy milk

INSTRUCTIONS

Put ¼ cup water or broth in the pressure cooker pot, press saute and add the chopped onion. Cook, stirring often until they begin to soften. Add garlic and continue to saute a few minutes.

Add the rest of the ingredients: spices, potatoes, carrots, and cabbage, the broth or water, and salt to taste.

Close the lid and cook on soup or manual for 20 minutes.

In the meantime, make the dumplings by mixing all of the ingredients in a bowl.

When the timer is done, and the pressure reduced, carefully open the pot. Add pepper to taste, and adjust salt.

Use the saute button again to keep the soup boiling so you can cook the dumplings.

Drop 1 tablespoonful each of the dumpling mixture into the boiling soup. Makes about 20. Don't make them too large as they expand when cooked.

Boil on medium-high for 6-10 minutes, flipping them half way through.

Stove-top INSTRUCTIONSs are basically the same, just check for doneness in the potatoes and carrots before dropping in the dumpling batter.

NUTRITION/NOTES

Amount Per Serving

Calories 180

Total Fat 0.8g1%

Total Carbohydrates 39.3g13%

Dietary Fiber 7.8g31%

Sugars 9.2g

Protein 6.5g13%

Calcium15%

Iron13%

234

The Carrot Soup

This Creamy Thai carrot soup made with a coconut curry vegetable broth, lite coconut milk smells so delightful you'll have to resist eating it all in one sitting.

Prep Time 15 minutes

Cook Time 15 minutes

Servings 4 people

1-1 1/2 cups

INGREDIENTS

1 medium yellow onion chopped

1 Tbl fresh ginger ,p eeled and grated

1 Tbl thai red curry paste add more to taste – can be foundthe Asian section of the store

2 cloves garlic peeled and chopped

1 lb carrots sliced (about 4 large)

3 cups low sodium vegetable broth plus more as needed. (or try homemade)

1 can light canned coconut milk 13.5-ounce

OR 1 tsp coconut extract mixed with 1 1/2 cups non-dairy milk

1-2 Tbl lime juice or lemon

2 Tbl fresh thymes leaves or cilantro minced

3/4 tsp sea salt (optional)

INSTRUCTIONS

In a large soup pot, water sauté the onion until it is soft.

Stir in the ginger, curry paste, and garlic and cook while stirring until well combined and fragrant, about 1 minute.

Add the carrots, stock, lime juice and bring to a boil over high heat. Reduce heat to low and simmer, covered, until the carrots are very tender, about 20 minutes.

Puree the soup in batches in a blender, using the hot fill line as a guide to reduce splatter.

Transfer the pureed soup back to the pot and place over low heat. Stir in the coconut milk and salt to taste. Simmer uncovered until the soup is heated through. Note: If the soup is not spicy enough, add more of the red curry paste. Serve with a sprinkling of thyme leaves.

NUTRITION/NOTES

Salt not included

Amount Per Serving

Calories 117

Total Fat 4g6%

Total Carbohydrates 19g6%

Dietary Fiber 5.6g22%

Sugars 10.7g

Protein 2.6g5%

Calcium7%

Iron7%

Tomato, Yam Soup

Servings 4 people

INGREDIENTS

1/2 large yellow onion chopped

2 cloves large garlic minced

239

8 oz. mushroom sliced

1/2 large red pepper chopped, or any color

1 large yam 1/4″ diced

1 14oz. can chopped tomatoes

1 cup baby spinach or chard or kale

1 head bok choy sliced

4 cups low sodium vegetable broth (or 4 cups homemade)

1/4 cup peanut butter

2 small chipotle peppers in adobo sauce, seeds removed

1 1/2 tsp ground coriander

1/2 tsp ground ginger or 1/2 Tbl. minced fresh

1/2 tsp sea salt (or to taste)

To Your Health Tomato, Yam Soup

INSTRUCTIONS

In a large soup pot, saute the chopped onion, garlic, mushroom, and pepper in a little water for a few minutes, then add the chopped yam and continue to saute for another 5-10 minutes.

Add the vegetable stock along with the chopped tomatoes and the spices (coriander, ground ginger, chipotle peppers or cayenne, salt).

When the vegetable become soft, add the bok choy and spinach and stir to combine.

Combine the peanut butter and about 1 cup of the stock in a small bowl and stir until well combined. Add to the soup pot and stir and continue to cook until the greens are done.

NUTRITION/NOTES

Amount Per Serving

Calories 167

Total Fat 7.5g12%

Total Carbohydrates 22.1g7%

Dietary Fiber 5.8g23%

Sugars 6.7g

Protein 6.8g14%

Calcium10%

Iron10%

Butternut Squash Panzanella Salad

Total Time
Prep: 25 min. Bake: 20 min.

Makes
8 servings

Ingredients

6 cups cubed day-old French bread (bite-sized cubes)

3 tablespoons olive oil

1/2 teaspoon chili powder

1/4 teaspoon salt

SALAD:

4 cups cubed peeled butternut squash (1-1/2-inch cubes)

1-1/2 cups sliced fresh mushrooms

1/2 cup olive oil, divided

1/2 teaspoon salt, divided

1/2 teaspoon pepper, divided

6 cups fresh arugula or fresh baby spinach

6 tablespoons sherry vinegar

3 shallots, thinly sliced

1/2 cup salted roasted almonds

6 tablespoons crumbled goat cheese

Directions

Preheat oven to 400°. Toss bread cubes with oil, chili powder and salt. Spread evenly in an ungreased 15x10x1-in. baking pan. Bake until golden brown, about 5 minutes. Transfer to a large bowl; cool.

In another large bowl, combine squash and mushrooms. Add 2 tablespoons oil, 1/4 teaspoon salt and 1/4 teaspoon pepper; toss to coat. Transfer to a greased 15x10x1-in. baking pan. Roast until tender, 20-25 minutes, stirring occasionally.

243

Add arugula and squash mixture to toasted bread. In a small bowl, whisk together vinegar, shallots and remaining oil, salt and pepper. Drizzle over salad; toss gently to combine. Top with almonds and goat cheese. Serve immediately.

Nutrition Facts

3/4 cup: 361 calories, 26g fat (4g saturated fat), 7mg cholesterol, 435mg sodium, 29g carbohydrate (5g sugars, 4g fiber), 7g protein.

Parsnip and Potato Gratin

Total Time
Prep: 20 min. Bake: 50 min.

Makes
8 servings

Ingredients

1 pound medium carrots, thinly sliced

1/2 pound medium parsnips, peeled and thinly sliced

1/2 pound Yukon Gold potatoes, peeled and thinly sliced

1 small onion, halved and sliced

2 garlic cloves, minced

1-1/2 teaspoons minced fresh rosemary

1/2 teaspoon salt

1/2 teaspoon ground nutmeg

1 cup half-and-half cream

1/4 cup heavy whipping cream

Directions

Preheat oven to 400°. In a large bowl, combine all ingredients. Transfer to a greased 3-qt. baking dish. Cover and bake until vegetables are tender, 40-45 minutes. Uncover and bake until cream has thickened and is beginning to turn golden brown, 10-15 minutes longer. Let stand 5-10 minutes before serving.

Nutrition Facts

3/4 cup: 141 calories, 6g fat (4g saturated fat), 23mg cholesterol, 208mg sodium, 19g carbohydrate (6g sugars, 3g fiber), 3g protein.

Asparagus Ham Dinner

Total Time

Prep/Total Time: 25 min.

Makes: 6 servings

Ingredients

2 cups uncooked corkscrew or spiral pasta

3/4 pound fresh asparagus, cut i nto 1-inch pieces

1 medium sweet yellow pepper, julienned

1 tablespoon olive oil

6 medium tomatoes, diced

6 ounces boneless fully cooked ham, cubed

1/4 cup minced fresh parsley

1/2 teaspoon salt

1/2 teaspoon dried oregano

1/2 teaspoon dried basil

1/8 to 1/4 teaspoon cayenne pepper

1/4 cup shredded Parmesan cheese

Directions

Cook pasta according to package INSTRUCTIONSs. Meanwhile, in a large cast-iron or other heavy skillet, saute asparagus and yellow pepper in oil until crisp-tender. Add tomatoes and ham; heat through. Drain pasta; add to vegetable mixture. Stir in parsley and seasonings. Sprinkle with cheese.

Nutrition Facts

1-1/3 cups: 204 calories, 5g fat (1g saturated fat), 17mg cholesterol, 561mg sodium, 29g carbohydrate (5g sugars, 3g fiber), 12g protein. Diabetic exchanges: 1-1/2 starch, 1 lean meat, 1 vegetable, 1/2 fat.

Autumn Harvest Pumpkin Pie

Total Time

Prep: 30 min. + chilling Bake: 55 min. + cooling

Makes

8 servings

Ingredients

250

2 cups all-purpose flour

1 cup cake flour

2 tablespoons sugar

1/2 teaspoon salt

1/2 cup cold unsalted butter, cubed

1/2 cup butter-flavored shortening

1 large egg

1/3 cup cold water

1 tablespoon cider vinegar

FILLING:

2-1/2 cups canned pumpkin (about 19 ounces)

1-1/4 cups packed light brown sugar

3/4 cup half-and-half cream

2 large eggs

1/4 cup apple butter

2 tablespoons orange juice

2 tablespoons maple syrup

2 teaspoons ground cinnamon

2 teaspoons pumpkin pie spice

1/4 teaspoon salt

Directions

In a large bowl, mix first 4 ingredients; cut in butter and shortening until crumbly. Whisk together egg, water and vinegar; gradually add to flour mixture, tossing with a fork until dough holds together when pressed. Divide dough in half so that one portion is slightly larger than the other; shape each into a disk. Wrap in plastic; refrigerate 1 hour or overnight.

Preheat oven to 425°. On a lightly floured surface, roll larger portion to a 1/8-in.-thick circle; transfer to a 9-in. deep-dish pie plate. Trim pastry to 1/2 in. beyond edge of pie plate. Refrigerate until ready to fill.

Roll smaller portion of dough to 1/8-in. thickness. Cut with a floured pumpkin-shaped cookie cutter; place some cutouts 1 in. apart on a baking sheet, reserving unbaked cutouts for decorative edge if desired. Bake until golden brown, 8-10 minutes.

Meanwhile, beat together filling ingredients until blended; transfer to crust. flute or decorate edge with unbaked cutouts, brushing off flour before pressing lightly onto edge. Bake on a lower oven rack 10 minutes. Cover edge loosely with foil. Reduce oven setting to 350°. Bake until a knife inserted near the center comes out clean, 45-50 minutes.

Cool on a wire rack; serve or refrigerate within 2 hours. Top with baked pumpkin cutouts before serving.

Editor's Note

This recipe was tested with commercially prepared apple butter.

Nutrition Facts

1 piece: 647 calories, 28g fat (12g saturated fat), 112mg cholesterol, 277mg sodium, 89g carbohydrate (47g sugars, 4g fiber), 9g protein.

Warm Cabbage, Fennel and Pear Salad

Total Time

Prep/Total Time: 25 min.

Makes

4 servings

Ingredients

2 firm medium pears

1/4 cup brandy or Cognac, optional

3 tablespoons olive oil

1 large fennel bulb, halved, cored and thinly sliced

4 cups shredded or thinly sliced cabbage

1/4 cup water

3 tablespoons lemon juice

2 teaspoons honey or agave nectar

1 teaspoon kosher salt

1/2 teaspoon pepper

3/4 cup crumbled or sliced Gorgonzola cheese

1/2 cup chopped walnuts, toasted

Directions

Peel and core pears; cut into 1/2-in. slices. If desired, toss with brandy. Set pears aside.

In a large skillet, heat oil over medium-high heat. Add fennel; saute until crisp-tender, 2-3 minutes. Add cabbage; toss with fennel. Cook until both are tender, 2-3 minutes longer. Add pears, water, lemon juice, honey, salt and pepper to skillet, gently combining ingredients. Cook until liquid is evaporated, 6-8 minutes.

Transfer to a serving bowl. Top with Gorgonzola cheese and toasted walnuts. Serve warm or at room temperature.

Test Kitchen Tips

If you choose not to use brandy or cognac, toss the pears in 1 tablespoon lemon juice to preserve their color and freshness.

Editor's Note

To toast nuts, bake in a shallow pan in a 350° oven for 5-10 minutes or cook in a skillet over low heat until lightly browned, stirring occasionally.

Nutrition Facts

1 cup: 391 calories, 26g fat (7g saturated fat), 19mg cholesterol, 810mg sodium, 28g carbohydrate (14g sugars, 8g fiber), 9g protein.

This scrumptious casserole combines pumpkin and two other kinds of squash in a creamy, savory mix. The recipe also would work with other squash combos, or just one type instead of three.

Total Time
Prep: 1-1/4 hours Bake: 35 min.

Makes
12 servings (3/4 cup each)

Ingredients

1 medium pie pumpkin (3 pounds)

1 medium butternut squash (3 pounds)

1 medium acorn squash (1-1/2 pounds)

1/4 cup sugar

1/4 cup maple syrup

1/4 cup butter, softened

1/2 teaspoon salt

1/2 teaspoon ground cinnamon

TOPPING:

1/2 cup all-purpose flour

1/2 cup packed brown sugar

1/2 cup old-fashioned oats

1/2 cup cold butter, cubed

1/2 cup chopped walnuts

Directions

Preheat oven to 400°. Cut pumpkin and squashes in half lengthwise; discard seeds or save for toasting. Place pumpkin and squashes in two greased 15x10x1-in. baking pans, cut side down. Bake, uncovered, 40-50 minutes or until tender.

Cool slightly; scoop out pulp and place in a large bowl. Mash pulp with sugar, maple syrup, butter, salt and cinnamon. Transfer to a greased 13x9-in. baking dish. In a small bowl, mix flour, brown sugar and oats; cut in butter until crumbly. Stir in walnuts.

Sprinkle over squash mixture. Bake, uncovered, 35-40 minutes or until bubbly and topping is golden brown.

Test Kitchen tips

If you have an electric pressure cooker, you can make quick work of cooking all the squash. Just a few minutes in there and you're ready to go.

While this is great with three different kinds of squash, feel free to use whatever combination you may have or just go with one single variety.

Nutrition Facts

3/4 cup: 337 calories, 15g fat (8g saturated fat), 31mg cholesterol, 201mg sodium, 51g carbohydrate (23g sugars, 6g fiber), 5g protein.

Quickpea Curry

This colorful curry is a nice change of pace for a busy weeknight. I like to substitute fresh peas for frozen when they're in season.

Total Time
Prep: 15 min. Cook: 35 min.

Makes
6 servings

Ingredients

1 tablespoon canola oil

1 medium onion, finely chopped

2 garlic cloves, minced

1 tablespoon curry powder

2 cans (14-1/2 ounces each) diced tomatoes, undrained

2 cans (15 ounces each) chickpeas or garbanzo beans, rinsed and drained

2 cups cubed peeled sweet potato (about 1 medium)

1 cup light coconut milk

2 teaspoons sugar

1/4 teaspoon crushed red pepper flakes

1 cup uncooked whole wheat pearl (Israeli) couscous

1-1/2 cups frozen peas (about 6 ounces)

1/4 teaspoon salt

Chopped fresh parsley

Plain yogurt, optional

Directions

In a large skillet, heat oil over medium heat; saute onion and garlic with curry powder until tender, 3-4 minutes. Stir in tomatoes, chickpeas, sweet potato, coconut milk, sugar and pepper flakes; bring to a boil. Reduce heat; simmer, uncovered, until mixture is thickened and potatoes are tender, 25-30 minutes, stirring occasionally.

Meanwhile, prepare couscous and peas separately according to package directions. Stir salt into peas.

To serve, divide couscous among 6 bowls. Top with chickpea mixture, peas, parsley and, if desired, yogurt.

Test Kitchen tips

Leftover coconut milk can be frozen or stirred into oatmeal or herbal tea, or even added to whisked eggs before scrambling them for a soft, fluffy version.

If you don't have pearl couscous on hand, regular couscous can be substituted.

Nutrition Facts

1 serving: 390 calories, 8g fat (2g saturated fat), 0 cholesterol, 561mg sodium, 68g carbohydrate (14g sugars, 13g fiber), 13g protein.

Red, White and Blueberry Pie

This creamy pie gets dressed up with berries to make a showstopping display at any Fourth of July party or summer get-together. It's as pretty as it is tasty!

Total Time

Prep: 20 min. + chilling

Makes

8 servings

Ingredients

2 ounces white baking chocolate, melted

One 9-inch graham cracker crust (about 6 ounces)

3/4 cup sliced fresh strawberries

1 package (8 ounces) cream cheese, softened

3/4 cup confectioners' sugar

3/4 cup 2% milk

1 package (3.3 ounces) instant white chocolate pudding mix

1 cup whipped topping

8 fresh strawberries, halved lengthwise

1 cup fresh blueberries

Directions

Spread melted chocolate onto bottom and sides of crust. Arrange sliced strawberries over chocolate.

In a bowl, beat cream cheese and confectioners' sugar until smooth; gradually beat in milk. Add pudding mix; beat on low speed until thickened, about 2 minutes. Spread over strawberries. Decorate pie with whipped topping, blueberries and halved strawberries. Refrigerate until serving.

Nutrition Facts

1 piece: 383 calories, 19g fat (10g saturated fat), 30mg cholesterol, 395mg sodium, 50g carbohydrate (44g sugars, 1g fiber), 4g protein.

Root Vegetable Pave

Total Time

Prep: 40 min. Bake: 1-3/4 hours + standing

Makes

8 servings

Ingredients

3 medium russet potatoes, peeled

2 large carrots

2 medium turnips, peeled

1 large onion, halved

1 medium fennel bulb, fronds reserved

1/2 cup all-purpose flour

1 cup heavy whipping cream

1 tablespoon minced fresh thyme, plus more for topping

1 tablespoon minced fresh rosemary

1/2 teaspoon salt

1/2 teaspoon pepper, plus more for topping

1 cup shredded Asiago cheese, divided

Directions

Preheat oven to 350°. With a mandoline or vegetable peeler, cut the first 5 ingredients into very thin slices. Transfer to a large bowl; toss with flour. Stir in the cream, thyme, 1 tablespoon rosemary, salt and pepper.

Place half of the vegetable mixture into a greased 9-in. springform pan. Sprinkle with 1/2 cup cheese. Top with remaining vegetable mixture. Place pan on a baking sheet and cover with a double thickness of foil.

Bake until vegetables are tender and easily pierced with a knife, 1-3/4 to 2 hours. Remove from oven and top foil with large canned goods as weights. Let stand 1 hour. Remove cans, foil and rim from pan before cutting. Top with remaining cheese. Add reserved fennel fronds and, as desired, additional fresh thyme and pepper. Refrigerate leftovers.

Nutrition Facts

265

1 slice: 248 calories, 15g fat (9g saturated fat), 46mg cholesterol, 216mg sodium, 23g carbohydrate (4g sugars, 2g fiber), 7g protein.

Total Time

Prep: 25 min. Bake: 20 min.

Makes

6 slices

Ingredients

1-1/2 to 1-3/4 cups white whole wheat flour

1-1/2 teaspoons baking powder

1/4 teaspoon salt

1/4 teaspoon each dried basil, oregano and parsley flakes

3/4 cup beer or nonalcoholic beer

TOPPINGS:

1-1/2 teaspoons olive oil

1 garlic clove, minced

2 cups shredded Italian cheese blend

2 cups fresh baby spinach

1 can (14 ounces) water-packed quartered artichoke hearts, drained and coarsely chopped

2 medium tomatoes, seeded and coarsely chopped

2 tablespoons thinly sliced fresh basil

Directions

Preheat oven to 425°. In a large bowl, whisk 1-1/2 cups flour, baking powder, salt and dried herbs until blended. Add beer, stirring just until moistened.

Turn dough onto a well-floured surface; knead gently 6-8 times, adding more flour if needed. Press dough to fit a greased 12-in. pizza pan. Pinch edge to form a rim. Bake until edge is lightly browned, about 8 minutes.

Mix oil and garlic; spread over crust. Sprinkle with 1/2 cup cheese; layer with spinach, artichoke hearts and tomatoes. Sprinkle with remaining cheese. Bake until crust is golden and cheese is melted, 8-10 minutes. Sprinkle with fresh basil.

Nutrition Facts

1 slice: 290 calories, 10g fat (6g saturated fat), 27mg cholesterol, 654mg sodium, 32g carbohydrate (1g sugars, 5g fiber), 14g protein. Diabetic Exchanges: 2 starch, 1 medium-fat meat, 1 vegetable.

Breadstick Pizza

Total Time

Prep: 25 min. Bake: 20 min.

Makes

12 servings

Ingredients

2 tubes (11 ounces each) refrigerated breadsticks

1/2 pound sliced fresh mushrooms

2 medium green peppers, chopped

1 medium onion, chopped

1-1/2 teaspoons Italian seasoning, divided

4 teaspoons olive oil, divided

1-1/2 cups shredded cheddar cheese, divided

5 ounces Canadian bacon, chopped

1-1/2 cups shredded part-skim mozzarella cheese

Marinara sauce

Directions

Unroll breadsticks into a greased 15x10x1-in. baking pan. Press onto the bottom and up the sides of pan; pinch seams to seal. Bake at 350° until set, 6-8 minutes.

Meanwhile, in a large skillet, saute the mushrooms, peppers, onion and 1 teaspoon Italian seasoning in 2 teaspoons oil until crisp-tender; drain.

Brush crust with remaining oil. Sprinkle with 3/4 cup cheddar cheese; top with vegetable mixture and Canadian bacon. Combine mozzarella cheese and remaining cheddar cheese; sprinkle over top. Sprinkle with remaining Italian seasoning.

Bake until cheese is melted and crust is golden brown, 20-25 minutes. Serve with marinara sauce.

Freeze option: Bake crust as directed, add toppings and cool. Securely wrap and freeze unbaked pizza. To use, unwrap pizza; bake as directed, increasing time as necessary.

Nutrition Facts

1 piece (calculated without marinara sauce): 267 calories, 11g fat (6g saturated fat), 27mg cholesterol, 638mg sodium, 29g carbohydrate (5g sugars, 2g fiber), 13g protein.

Prep Time: 10 Minutes

Serves: 8

Ingredients

4 oz. good quality cream cheese, at room temperature

1/4 cup unsalted butter, at room temperature

1/4 cup extra virgin coconut oil

2 Tbsp. Erythritol

3/4 cup fresh blueberries plus some for topping

1 Tbsp. Fresh lemon juice plus zest of 1 lemon

Instructions

Mix cream cheese, butter, coconut oil and erythritol until creamy

Using a high-speed blender blend the blueberries

Add blueberries, lemon juice and lemon zest to the cheese mixture and blend well

Spoon into mini muffins liners or silicone moulds and lightly press fresh blueberries into the cheesecake. Top with more lemon zest if you wish. Freeze until firm, about 2 hours. Remove from the liners and store in an airtight container. Keep frozen until ready to eat. Bring to room temperature for 15 minutes before serving

If you love a moist and creamy cake, this is it. Lemon juice and lemonade give the layers a tangy touch, and the cream cheese frosting with sprinkles makes it pretty.

Total Time
Prep: 50 min. Bake: 20 min. + cooling

Makes
12 servings

Ingredients

1 cup buttermilk

2 tablespoons lemon juice

2 tablespoons seedless strawberry jam, warmed

2 tablespoons thawed pink lemonade concentrate

2 tablespoons grenadine syrup

1 cup unsalted butter, softened

1-1/4 cups sugar

3 tablespoons grated lemon zest

4 large eggs, room temperature

1/2 teaspoon vanilla extract

2-1/2 cups all-purpose flour

1 teaspoon baking powder

1/2 teaspoon baking soda

1/2 teaspoon salt

FROSTING:

1 cup unsalted butter, softened

1 package (8 ounces) cream cheese, softened

1 tablespoon grated lemon zest

4 cups confectioners' sugar

1/3 cup plus 3 tablespoons thawed pink lemonade concentrate, divided

Pink sprinkles

Directions

Preheat oven to 350°. Line bottoms of three greased 8-in. round baking pans with parchment; grease paper.

In a small bowl, whisk the first 5 ingredients until blended. In a large bowl, cream butter, sugar and lemon zest until light and fluffy. Add eggs, one at a time, beating well after each addition. Beat in vanilla. In another bowl, whisk flour, baking powder, baking soda and salt; add to creamed mixture alternately with buttermilk mixture, beating well after each addition.

Transfer batter to prepared pans. Bake until a toothpick inserted in center comes out clean, 20-24 minutes. Cool in pans 10 minutes before removing to wire racks; remove paper. Cool completely.

For frosting, in a large bowl, beat butter, cream cheese and lemon zest until smooth. Gradually beat in confectioners' sugar and 1/3 cup lemonade concentrate. If necessary, refrigerate until spreadable, up to 1 hour.

Place 1 cake layer on a serving plate. Brush 1 tablespoon lemonade concentrate over cake; spread with 1/2 cup frosting. Repeat layers. Top with remaining cake layer; brush remaining lemonade concentrate over top.

Spread remaining frosting over top and sides of cake. Decorate with sprinkles. Refrigerate until serving.

For cupcakes: Make batter as directed; fill 24 paper-lined muffin cups three-fourths full. Bake in a preheated 350° oven for 16-19 minutes or until a toothpick comes out clean. Cool in pans 10 minutes before removing to wire racks to cool completely. Prepare frosting as directed, omitting 3 tablespoons lemonade concentrate for brushing layers; pipe or spread frosting over tops. Yield: 2 dozen cupcakes.

Nutrition Facts

1 slice: 732 calories, 39g fat (24g saturated fat), 172mg cholesterol, 291mg sodium, 91g carbohydrate (68g sugars, 1g fiber), 7g protein.

Total Time

Prep: 25 min. + chilling Bake: 15 min. + cooling

Makes

18 mini pies

Ingredients

3 tablespoons quick-cooking tapioca

4 cups sliced fresh strawberries

2 cups sliced fresh rhubarb

3/4 cup sugar

1 teaspoon grated orange zest

1 teaspoon vanilla extract

1/4 teaspoon salt

1/4 teaspoon ground cinnamon

3 drops red food coloring, optional

Pastry for double-crust pie (9 inches)

Directions

Preheat oven to 425°. Place tapioca in a small food processor or spice grinder; process until finely ground.

In a large saucepan, combine strawberries, rhubarb, sugar, orange zest, vanilla, salt, cinnamon, tapioca and, if desired, food coloring; bring to a boil. Reduce heat; simmer, covered, 15-20 minutes or until strawberries are tender, stirring occasionally. Transfer to a large bowl; cover and refrigerate overnight.

On a lightly floured surface, roll one half of dough to an 18-in. circle. Cut 12 circles with a 4-in. biscuit cutter, rerolling scraps as necessary; press dough onto bottom and up sides of ungreased muffin cups. Cut 6 more circles with remaining dough. Spoon strawberry mixture into muffin cups.

Bake 12-15 minutes or until filling is bubbly and crust golden brown. Cool in pan 5 minutes; remove to wire racks to cool.

Pastry for double-crust pie (9 inches): Combine 2-1/2 cups all-purpose flour and 1/2 tsp. salt; cut in 1 cup cold butter until crumbly. Gradually add 1/3 to 2/3 cup ice water, tossing with a fork until dough holds together when pressed. Divide dough in half. Shape each into a disk; wrap in plastic wrap. Refrigerate 1 hour or overnight.

Nutrition Facts

1 mini pie: 207 calories, 10g fat (6g saturated fat), 27mg cholesterol, 171mg sodium, 27g carbohydrate (11g sugars, 1g fiber), 2g protein.

Total Time

Prep: 15 min. + chilling Bake: 10 min. + cooling

Makes

10 cookies

Ingredients

1 cup all-purpose flour

1/2 cup old-fashioned or quick-cooking oats

1/3 cup packed brown sugar

2 teaspoons grated lemon zest

1/2 teaspoon grated whole nutmeg or 1 teaspoon ground nutmeg

1/2 teaspoon salt

3/4 cup cold butter, cubed

2 tablespoons heavy cream

1 teaspoon vanilla extract

1/2 cup cinnamon baking chips

10 tablespoons Biscoff creamy cookie spread

20 large marshmallows

Directions

Place the first six ingredients in a food processor; process until blended. Add butter, cream and vanilla; pulse until dough comes together (do not overmix). Stir in cinnamon chips. Divide dough in half. Shape each into a disk; wrap and refrigerate until firm enough to roll, about 30 minutes.

Preheat oven to 350°. On a lightly floured surface, roll each portion of dough to 1/4-in. thickness. Cut with a floured 2-1/2-in. square cookie cutter. Place 1 in. apart on ungreased baking sheets. Bake until cookies begin to brown, 10-12 minutes (do not overbake). Remove from pans to wire racks to cool completely.

Preheat broiler. Spread 1 tablespoon cookie spread on bottoms of half of the cookies. Set aside. Place a marshmallow on bottoms of the remaining cookies; transfer to a baking sheet. Broil 5-6 in. from heat until marshmallows are golden brown, 30-45 seconds. Cover with cookie spread halves; press down gently.

Dessert Pizza

Total Time

Prep: 35 min. + chilling Bake: 15 min. + cooling

Makes

12-16 servings

Ingredients

1/4 cup butter, softened

1/2 cup sugar

1 large egg

1/4 teaspoon vanilla extract

1/4 teaspoon lemon extract

1-1/4 cups all-purpose flour

1/4 teaspoon baking powder

1/4 teaspoon baking soda

1/4 teaspoon salt

GLAZE:

1/4 cup sugar

2 teaspoons cornstarch

1/4 cup water

1/4 cup orange juice

TOPPING:

4 ounces cream cheese, softened

1/4 cup confectioners' sugar

1 cup whipped topping

1 firm banana, sliced

1 cup sliced fresh strawberries

1 can (8 ounces) mandarin oranges, drained

2 kiwifruit, peeled and thinly sliced

1/3 cup fresh blueberries

Directions

In a small bowl, cream butter and sugar until light and fluffy. Beat in egg and extracts. Combine flour, baking powder, baking soda and salt; add to creamed mixture and beat well. Cover and refrigerate for 30 minutes.

Press dough into a greased 12- to 14-in. pizza pan. Bake at 350°
for 12-14 minutes or until light golden brown. Cool completely on
a wire rack.

For glaze, combine sugar and cornstarch in a small saucepan. Stir
in the water and orange juice until smooth. Bring to a boil; cook
and stir for 1-2 minutes or until thickened. Cool to room
temperature, about 30 minutes.

For topping, in a small bowl, beat cream cheese and
confectioners' sugar until smooth. Add whipped topping; mix
well. Spread over crust. Arrange fruit on top. Brush glaze over
fruit. Store in the refrigerator.

Test Kitchen Tips

Use premade sugar cookie dough to save a bit of time.

If you're in a pinch, orange marmalade works in place of the glaze.

Nutrition Facts

1 piece: 176 calories, 7g fat (4g saturated fat), 29mg cholesterol,
118mg sodium, 27g carbohydrate (17g sugars, 1g fiber), 2g
protein.

Total Time
Prep: 30 min. + chilling

Makes
12 servings

Ingredients
32 soft ladyfingers, split

1 envelope unflavored gelatin

1/4 cup lime juice, chilled

2 packages (8 ounces each) cream cheese, softened

1 cup sugar

6 ounces white baking chocolate, melted and cooled

2 teaspoons grated lime zest

1 cup heavy whipping cream, whipped

Fresh strawberry and lime slices, optional

Directions

Arrange 20 ladyfingers around the edges and 12 ladyfingers on the bottom of an ungreased 8-in. springform pan; set aside. In a small saucepan, sprinkle gelatin over cold lime juice; let stand for 1 minute. Heat over low heat, stirring until gelatin is completely dissolved; cool.

Meanwhile, beat cream cheese and sugar until smooth. Gradually beat in melted chocolate, lime zest and gelatin mixture. Fold in whipped cream. Pour into prepared pan. Cover and refrigerate until set, about 3 hours. Remove sides of pan. If desired, garnish with strawberry and lime slices.

Nutrition Facts

1 slice: 408 calories, 25g fat (16g saturated fat), 100mg cholesterol, 267mg sodium, 42g carbohydrate (35g sugars, 0 fiber), 6g protein.

Total Time

Prep/Total Time: 20 min.

Makes

18 servings

Ingredients

2 packages (8 ounces each) cream cheese, softened

1/2 cup sugar

1/2 teaspoon vanilla extract

1/2 teaspoon almond extract

2 cups heavy whipping cream, whipped

2 quarts strawberries, halved, divided

2 quarts blueberries, divided

Directions

In a large bowl, beat cream cheese, sugar and extracts until fluffy. Fold in whipped cream. Place a third of the mixture in a 4-qt. bowl. Reserve 20 strawberry halves and 1/2 cup blueberries for garnish.

Layer half of the remaining strawberries and blueberries over cream mixture. Top with another third of the cream mixture and the remaining berries. Spread the remaining cream mixture on top. Use the reserved strawberries and blueberries to make a "flag" on top.

Nutrition Facts

1 cup: 168 calories, 10g fat (6g saturated fat), 32mg cholesterol, 44mg sodium, 20g carbohydrate (15g sugars, 3g fiber), 2g protein.

Kale Bruschetta

Ready In: 25 minutes

Makes 8 Pieces

We adore this as an appetizer, and so does everyone else. It is always the first empty platter at our holiday party. No one knows it is plant-based; they just know it is so yummy.

Ingredients

1 bunch kale

1 loaf fresh 100% whole-grain bread, sliced

½ cup Cannellini Bean Sauce

1 cup grape tomatoes, halved

balsamic glaze

Instructions

Place the kale leaves in a large pot of boiling water. Cover and cook until tender, about 5 minutes. Drain in a colander, then squeeze out any extra liquid with your hands (you don't want soggy bread).

Toast 8 pieces of bread, and place them on a handsome serving platter.

Spread a tablespoon of the Cannellini Bean Sauce on the toasted bread, then cover with a layer of kale and top with a scattering of grape tomatoes. Drizzle generously with the balsamic glaze, and grab one for yourself before they all disappear.

Vegan Quesadillas

Prep-time: 2 hours 15 minutes / Cook Time: 15 minutes

Serves 4

Ingredients

¾ cup raw cashews, soaked for 2 hours

½ cup nutritional yeast flakes

1 lime, juiced

½ tablespoon stoneground mustard, no-salt added

½ cup water

1 yellow onion, sliced thin

1 red bell pepper, sliced thin

1 yellow bell pepper, sliced thin

1½ tablespoons ground cumin

1½ teaspoon chili powder

8 100% corn tortillas, no salt or oil added

2 cups fresh spinach, loosely packed

Instructions

Make the cheese sauce: Add the cashews, nutritional yeast, lime, stoneground mustard and water to a blender. Blend until it the sauce is creamy. Set it aside.

Make the onion-pepper filling: Place a sauté pan over medium heat. Add the sliced onion and bell pepper. Stir in the cumin and chili powder. Cover and cook for 5 minutes, stirring occasionally so the veggies don't stick to the bottom of the pan. Then stir in a tablespoon of water and continue cooking uncovered. When the water evaporates stir in another tablespoon of water, continuing to sauté until the onions are caramelized.

Turn the heat to low. Pour the cheese sauce into the onion and peppers. Stir well and then cover with a lid so the mixture doesn't dry out.

Make the first quesadilla: Place a non-stick pan over medium heat. Let it heat for 5 minutes. Then place one of the tortillas into the pan. Set a timer, letting the first side toast for 2 minutes and then flip. Set the timer for another 2 minutes. As you wait, carefully scoop about ¼ of the filling onto the tortilla and spread it evenly, forming a single layer of peppers and onions. Layer ½ cup of spinach across the onions and peppers. Place the second tortilla on top of the spinach.

294

Once the timer goes off or the bottom side is toasted, use a large spatula to carefully flip the entire quesadilla. Toast the second tortilla for 2-3 minutes.

When the quesadilla is done transfer it to a plate. Repeat this process with the remaining filling to make a total of 4 quesadillas. Note that subsequent quesadillas may require less cooking time because the pan will be hotter. You may want to turn the heat down slightly after the first couple. Slice the quesadillas into triangular pieces and serve.

Chef's Note: Soaking the cashews softens them so they become creamy when blended. If you're using a high-powered blender such as a vitamix, the nuts do not need to be soaked.

Herbed Hummus

Prep-time: 20-25 minutes

Serves 8 (1 quart)

Ingredients

1 cup fresh basil leaves, lightly packed and blanched

½ cup fresh tarragon leaves, lightly packed and blanched

4 cups cooked garbanzo beans

1 cup vegetable broth

½ cup fresh flat-leaf parsley leaves, lightly packed

Juice of 1 lemon

2 tablespoons sesame seeds, toasted

2 cloves garlic

¼ cup chopped chives

Instructions

Pat the basil and tarragon dry and coarsely chop them. Transfer to a food processor. Add the beans, broth, parsley, lemon juice, sesame seeds, and garlic and process until the desired consistency is achieved. Stir in the chives. Stored in a sealed container in the refrigerator, Herbed Hummus will keep for 4 days.

Note: Most food processors don't do a good job of chopping chives, as the chives tend to get wound around the base of the blade. That's why I suggest you chop them by hand.

Smoky Little Devils

Makes 24

Ingredients

FOR THE HUMMUS:

1 (15-ounce) no-salt-added chickpeas, drained and rinsed

2 large cloves garlic

2 tablespoons fresh lemon juice

1½ tablespoons spicy brown mustard, or to taste

Freshly ground black pepper, to taste

¼ teaspoon salt (optional; we do not use it)

1 cup chopped green onions (4 to 5)

2 teaspoons Dijon mustard, or to taste

Zest of 1 lemon

1½ to 2 additional tablespoons fresh lemon juice, to taste

½ teaspoon ground turmeric

FOR THE DEVILS

12 small red potatoes (roughly the size of large walnuts or small clementines)

Pinch of smoked paprika, for garnish

1 green onion, finely sliced, for garnish

Baby kale leaves, for garnish (optional)

Green Onion Hummus

Instructions

To make Hummus, in a food processor, combine the chickpeas, garlic, lemon juice, mustard, pepper to taste, salt (if using), and 2 tablespoons water, and process until uniformly smooth.

In a small bowl, stir together the hummus, green onions, Dijon mustard, lemon zest, additional lemon juice, and turmeric. Dollop or spread on immediately or store in an airtight container until ready to use.

To make the Smoky Devils, set a steamer insert in a saucepan and add about 2 inches of water. Bring to a boil over high heat; then place the potatoes in the steamer basket and steam for about 20 minutes. Plunge them into cold water in a big bowl or just run cold water over them.

Slice each potato in half. With the small end of a melon-baller or a small spoon, scoop out a hole in the center. (Save the little scooped-out potato balls to put into a salad or just pop them into your mouth!)

Fill each hole with hummus. Sprinkle with smoked paprika. It is easiest to take a tiny bit between your fingers and sprinkle just enough for the color to show. Garnish with green onions or, for a really fun look, use a tiny baby kale leaf as a "sail" in each little potato "boat."

Herb-Crusted Asparagus Spears

Ready In: 40 minutes

Makes 4 Servings

Ingredients

1 bunch of asparagus (about 12 spears)

2 tablespoons hemp seeds

1/4 cup nutritional yeast

1 teaspoon garlic powder or 3 garlic cloves, minced

1/8 teaspoon ground pepper

Pinch of paprika

1/4 cup whole wheat breadcrumbs

Juice of ½ lemon

Instructions

Preheat the oven to 350°F.

Wash the asparagus. To remove the white bottom end, hold each asparagus spear with both hands and bend it near the white end. The white end will snap off.

Transfer hemp seeds to a small bowl and mix in the nutritional yeast, garlic, pepper, paprika, and breadcrumbs. Stir and set aside.

Arrange the asparagus spears side by side in a baking dish and sprinkle with the hemp mixture.

Bake for 20-25 minutes or until asparagus are crispy.

Serve and sprinkle with some lemon juice.

Prep-time: 25 minutes / Cook Time: 50 minutes

Makes 3-4 rolls

Ingredients

RICE INGREDIENTS:

1 cup organic short grain brown rice

1½ tablespoons organic rice vinegar

1 tablespoon evaporated cane sugar

¼ teaspoon sea salt

FILLING INGREDIENTS:

1 small Japanese yam, roasted

½ ripe avocado

1 carrot, cut into thin strips

½ cucumber, peeled and cut into thin strips

3-4 toasted nori sheets

¾ cup organic crispy brown rice cereal

½ cup pickled ginger

TERIYAKI SAUCE INGREDIENTS:

½ cup wheat-free organic tamari

⅓ cup evaporated cane sugar

2 teaspoons brown rice vinegar

2 teaspoons pickled ginger, diced

¼ teaspoon garlic powder

2 tablespoons pineapple juice

½ teaspoon yuzu juice (optional)

2 teaspoons arrowroot powder, plus 1 tablespoons water, whisked

Instructions

Roast Japanese yam at 375°F for 45 minutes, or until soft. Peel and dice when cool and set aside in bowl.

In a medium saucepan, add 2 cups water and rice and cook according to directions. When cooked, transfer rice into a large bowl. With a wooden paddle, incorporate vinegar, sugar and sea salt into rice until slightly sticky, stirring vigorously. Let cool. Set aside.

For teriyaki sauce: In small pot over medium heat add tamari, sugar, vinegar, ginger, garlic powder, pineapple juice and yuzu, if using. Whisk. Cook for about 3 minutes, add arrowroot slurry and whisk. Cook about 30 more seconds.

To roll sushi, place sheet of toasted nori (shiny side down) on roller. With damp hands, spread cooked rice evenly over nori, leaving ½ inch on top portion of nori bare. Sprinkle with generous helping of crispy rice cereal. Flip sushi over onto plastic wrap lined sushi roller.

Place small amount cooked yam, avocado, carrots and cucumber in a horizontal line, about 1 inch from base of nori.

Turn sushi roller with fillings vertical to your body and slowly lift sides of sushi roller while making small rocking motions to align fillings. Using roller, tuck in filling until completely closed, allowing remaining top 3 inches of nori with rice to be exposed. Now fully enclose roll and squeeze gently. Slowly rock sushi using roller, until it forms a round shape. Gently press to seal, and round out sushi. Slide onto clean surface, and with a serrated damp knife, cut into 1 inch thick slices. When serving, drizzle with teriyaki sauce. Serve with ginger.

Conclusion

Intermittent fasting may work amazingly well for some people, and terribly for others. Most importantly, if you do decide to give intermittent fasting a try, be sure to listen to your body's feedback. Easing into intermittent fasting by starting with shorter fasting windows can help with initial symptoms of hunger and discomfort. But if it becomes too uncomfortable, be honest with yourself, accept it, and move on.

At the end of the day, nothing can have a greater impact on your health than a diet consisting of real, whole foods, and a lifestyle that prioritizes your physical, mental, and emotional well-being.

I hope this book was able to help you to discover the right fasting method for you.

The next step is to apply what you have learned from this book by creating a fasting plan that would work with your current lifestyle and help you achieve your personal fitness goals.

You should also go for a consultation with your physician as well in order to get their opinion about your plan to fast. Make sure that you would be able to fully commit to fasting once you have begun. Though the planning stage may take a long time, you should push through until you are completely certain about the details pertaining to this life-changing decision.

I'd like to thank you and congratulate you for transiting my lines from start to finish.

I wish you the best of luck!

Lightning Source UK Ltd.
Milton Keynes UK
UKHW020810180121
377239UK00005B/99